PLAYING AWAY

Books by Michael Mewshaw

Nonfiction

Playing Away: Roman Holidays and Other
    Mediterranean Encounters   *1988*
Money to Burn: The True Story of the Benson
    Family Murders   *1987*
Short Circuit   *1983*
Life for Death   *1980*

Fiction

Blackballed   *1986*
Year of the Gun   *1984*
Land Without Shadow   *1979*
Earthly Bread   *1976*
The Toll   *1974*
Waking Slow   *1972*
Man in Motion   *1970*

PLAYING AWAY

◆ ◆ ◆ ◆ ◆ ◆ ◆

Roman Holidays and Other
Mediterranean Encounters

MICHAEL MEWSHAW

◆ ◆ ◆ ◆ ◆ ◆ ◆

An Owl Book
Henry Holt and Company / New York

Copyright © 1988 by Michael Mewshaw
Published by Henry Holt and Company, Inc.,
115 West 18th Street, New York, New York 10011.

Library of Congress Cataloging-in-Publication Data
Mewshaw, Michael, 1943–
    Playing away : Roman holidays and other Mediterranean encounters /
Michael Mewshaw.—1st Owl Book ed.
    p.   cm.
"An Owl book."
ISBN 0-8050-1225-7 (pbk.)
1. Mewshaw, Michael, 1943–   —Journeys—Mediterranean Region.
2. Mediterranean Region—Description and travel.   3. Italy—
Civilization—20th century.   4. Authors, American—20th century—Biography.   I. Title.
[PS3563.E87Z47   1990]
818'.5403—dc20
[B]   89-24569
                                                                           CIP

Henry Holt books are available at special discounts
for bulk purchases for sales promotions, premiums,
fund-raising, or educational use. Special editions
or book excerpts can also be created to specification.

        For details contact:

        Special Sales Director
        Henry Holt and Company, Inc.
        115 West 18th Street
        New York, New York 10011

First published in hardcover by Atheneum in 1988.
First Owl Book Edition—1990
Printed in the United States of America
10 9 8 7 6 5 4 3 2 1

Portions of this book appeared, in a slightly different form,
in *European Travel & Life* magazine.

For Desmond O'Grady
and Marcia and Stefano Starace
and Tom Carney and Maureen Lambrey

"Living in a foreign country
is like being on a football
team without a home field.
You're always playing away."
—Desmond O'Grady
    Australian writer and
    longtime resident of Rome

• • • • •

CONTENTS

CONTENTS

INTRODUCTION

Settle in Seattle or Sheboygan; Los Angeles or Las Cruces; Chicago or Carbondale; Miami, Ohio, or Miami, Florida; and you never have to justify your decision. But if you're an American living in Europe, you learn to expect to be asked, Why?

Recently I've taken to cribbing a line from Gore Vidal. Pressed to explain how he came to spend half his life in Rome, Vidal replied that the question put him in mind of the late Howard Hughes, who when people demanded why he lived isolated in a darkened hotel room, his hair hanging uncut to his shoulders, his fingernails five inches long, his feet shod in Kleenex boxes, said, "Oh, it's just something I drifted into."

Generally, that gets a laugh or, at least, gets the inquisitor off the subject. But still if, as Gertrude Stein wrote, remarks aren't literature, it's equally true that wisecracks aren't explanations. And so the mystery remains: Why?

Sometimes the question sounds almost like an accusation or an insult, as if anybody who chose not to stay in his own country with his fellow citizens were automatically suspect. An editor, an Amherst College graduate no less, recently wondered if I was still an American. She thought you lost your passport if you lived outside the United States too long.

For those who cannot imagine a good reason for leaving home, it seems to be an easy leap to the conclusion that there must be a bad one. Drink? Drugs? A gaudy secret vice or twisted political belief? At best, expatriates are seen as trying to cure one form of alienation with another. At worst . . . well, fill in the blank. The list of bleak possibilities is endless.

While it is never pleasant—never less than an impertinence—to be pressured by somebody else to justify your life, a writer owes it to himself to try to understand the decisions that have shaped his character, his career, his very consciousness. For me and for my work, place is of crucial importance, but where one lives and travels is a bit like marriage in that the reasons that seemed so urgent during the honeymoon scarcely apply as years pass, children arrive, atoms rearrange themselves, and gravity exerts its inexorable pull. In short, I always had a reason for living overseas. It's just that the reason kept changing.

Twenty years ago, I came to Europe because the Fulbright Commission was deluded into thinking I spoke French and meant to write a ruminative historical novel about the relationship between Paul Verlaine and Arthur Rimbaud. Instead, I completed a picaresque tale about a driving trip to Mexico. In the era of *Easy Rider,* it was an anti-road novel.

Then I went on the road myself, traveling through England, Italy, Spain, Portugal, Morocco, Greece, Egypt, Lebanon, and Turkey. Without much reflection, I viewed this as what an aspiring writer was supposed to do—see life in the raw, eat on the cheap, take risks (mostly to my alimentary tract), and meet people. In some inchoate way, I equated curiosity with creativity, mileage covered with imagination improved.

After a brief stint of teaching in the States, I returned for a longer stay in Europe and North Africa. The decisive factor was free time. Life abroad was cheap, there were fewer intrusions from friends and enemies alike, and I had the sense that I had checked into a colorful, cut-rate *pensione*. It wasn't quite real; I couldn't yet conceive of settling here permanently. But its influence had begun to insinuate itself into my fiction and I longed to deal with a world wider than that of my first two autobiographical novels.

Graham Greene has written that an author's childhood is the bank account he draws on for the rest of his career; essentially he sustains himself on the patrimony he came into as a kid. This may be so. I suspected it was true and feared I had been shortchanged. I wanted to switch banks or start pilfering from somebody else's safe-deposit box. It didn't matter whether it held more or less money than mine, just so long as it was in a different currency. Better yet, I hoped to break out of a familiar accounting system and into a more challenging calculus.

After another interval of teaching, I settled in Rome and used it as a base where I left my wife and son while I went off to the Sahara to do research for a few novels—two tragic, one comic. By now Europe seemed less like a *pensione* and more like home. It was becoming increasingly difficult to check out and move back to where we theoretically belonged.

Interestingly, although our families and friends and even utter strangers persisted in asking Why?, Italians took it for granted that we would want to live here. They naturally assumed that anybody who appreciated art, history, good wine, mild weather, marvelous food, proximity to the mountains and the sea, and incessant *commedia dell'arte* in the streets would choose Rome.

Still, I confess, even as I put down tentative roots, listening as my two sons swiftly outstripped my grasp of the language, I harbored ambivalent feelings and wondered whether and when we should leave. I rented a series of furnished apartments, kept my kids in American schools, never really feathered my nest, never acknowledged that the move was permanent. I existed—and after a decade still do —in a state of anticipation, of pure contingency, like those illegal aliens in the United States who keep their commitments and possessions to a minimum and are always ready to run for the border. This doesn't strike me as an altogether inadvisable state of alert for a writer to maintain anywhere in the world.

Historically, Italy has often provoked mixed emotions in Americans, and although it attracted artists and writers, something about its easy sensuality or overripe charm seemed to frighten them. Authors as radically different as Nathaniel Hawthorne and Tennessee Williams imagined a witch's brew of evil bubbling up out of contradictory ingredients—religious intolerance and Mediterranean amorality.

Arriving in Rome in 1869, dizzied by the city's splendor, Henry James scrawled in his notebook, "At last, for the first time, I live." But he didn't stay; he moved on to London. More revealing, he filled his fiction with characters who did remain in Rome only to be morally corrupted, artistically destroyed, financially ruined, physically maimed, or flat-out killed.

Even today, Rome is alternately viewed as a museum or a mausoleum. When not described as dirty, disorderly, or dangerous, it is dismissed as culturally dead.

If these reactions to Rome sound mercurial, maybe it's because the city itself is notoriously fickle, elusive, and volatile. For centuries people have pointed out that nothing here is what it seems to be, but I think it would be more accurate to observe that nothing is entirely what it appears to be at the moment. Everything is in transition. I am not talking now about slow evolutions over eons or about the way that famous palaces have metamorphosed into hotels, or churches have changed into supper clubs, or the Via Veneto has gone from chic to glitz to kitsch. I am referring to the alterations Rome undergoes from hour to hour, from afternoon to evening. An open-air market folds its stands and is replaced by restaurant tables; a fountain becomes a footbath or a car wash; arches in the Aurelian Wall turn into storage sheds and sturdy garages; lovers sit and kiss, then eventually stretch out full-length on the ledge in front of the French Embassy, apparently convinced of their impregnability under the watchful eyes of armed guards and the automatic cameras that pan the Piazza Farnese.

Although the city is no longer a center of commerce or any contemporary art, I find it a good spot to live and work. Small enough to cross on foot, friendly but never nosy, it's an easy place to meet people or to avoid them. It's also close to other cities and countries that are equally fascinating.

Of course, Rome is no longer cheap. It costs as much as or more than any American city, including New York. Yet it still offers stage sets and dramatic tableaux that cannot be equaled for any price at La Scala or the Metropolitan.

I like seeing boys playing soccer under the portico of the Pantheon. I relish those squares where a painted grid of lines and an enterprising old man with a cap have turned an august piazza into a parking lot. I enjoy evenings when great flocks of swifts wheel against the sky, circumflexes of black flickering against a surface of blue. I'm entranced by the columns that erupt from the pavement on Via del Portico d'Ottavia like ancient buried secrets bursting through the smug veneer of the modern city to remind passersby that there is no end, no final explanation to this town.

Finally, though, it is not so much this miscellany of sights and impressions that holds me here as it is the exemplary tales which Italy and the entire Mediterranean basin provide with the same spendthrift profusion as they produce flowers in every season, music for every emotion, and obscenities that help cancel out every frustration. Some of these anecdotes are collected in this volume, and I trust they will offer a satisfactory answer to the inevitable question, Why do you stay over there?

They cannot pretend to tell the whole tale—neither of my life nor of the places I've lived. Generally lighthearted, they treat some of the same subjects I've dealt with in my fiction, but come at them from a different direction. Other themes that have shaped my novels—terrorism, political intrigue, violence—appear only glancingly. Perhaps this shows that what dominates a writer's unconscious mind and imagination doesn't necessarily dominate his daily life and his nonfiction. Or maybe it indicates that events which start off as tragedy can, as Marx said of history, repeat themselves as comedy, if not farce. The reverse, of course, is also possible.

In any case, I don't regard these pieces as conventional travel writing, chock-a-block with recommendations for hotels, restaurants, and tourist attractions which, miraculously, show up in brochures free of beggars, cripples, cars, smog, graffiti, and garbage. If anything, the book is a kind of anti-tourist guide or piecemeal biography that attempts to convey what it has been like for me and other expatriates —some obscure, some celebrated—to stay put in spots which most people see only as they pass through. It would be a mistake to describe us as Janus-faced; we don't stare constantly in opposite directions—toward home and here. But we unavoidably view present surroundings through eyes that have seen other places. We are in the contradictory position of playing away—both enjoying ourselves and groping for surer footing on a foreign field.

If the picture occasionally seems full of warts and the tone impatient, even irascible, blame the author, not the places. It is, in my opinion, imperfections in places, no less than in people, that make them worth writing and reading about.

PLAYING AWAY

♦ ♦ ♦ ♦ ♦

ITALY, 1977

When they heard I was headed for Italy, several French agencies refused to rent me a car. I had no luck until I located an outfit in Nice that had a Fiat that needed to be returned to Rome. After I had signed the papers, the officious agent in a red company blazer came with me to the parking lot to demonstrate the intricacies of the double-lock mechanism.

Two keys were linked by a long jangling chain, and the man had to strain mightily to insert one key under the dashboard before putting the other into the ignition.

"Remember," he said, "turn the left key first. Then the right. Now you practice."

While I tested my ambidexterity, he told me that Italians steal everything and dramatized his point by repeating a story, perhaps apocryphal, which had made international news. Twenty-two or thirty-four German dentists—the number varied according to which wire service one read—had driven to a convention in Milan. Eighteen of them, Mercedes owners all, returned to Germany without their cars.

I was in a hurry and said so, but the agent insisted on showing me the trunk. He hoped it would hold all my belongings. If I left anything in the backseat, "they" were sure to smash the windows and swipe it.

I assured him my luggage would fit. In the backseat, there would be a baby stroller, a crib, and a few toys—nothing to interest even the most desperate thief.

The man was astounded. "You have a child?"

I nodded that I did.

"You're taking a baby to Italy?" he asked, incredulous.

I admitted I was.

"Don't you read the papers? Don't you watch television? Don't you know what's happening there?" He flung an arm in the direction of the Italian border, less than thirty miles away, and spoke as if we were near the front line of a fierce battle. He went on to talk of chaos, of crazy students in the streets, kidnappings, killings.

Cutting him short, I slid behind the wheel, turned the left-hand key, then the right, and drove home to pack. But something of the agent's high-frequency hysteria must have unhinged me, for two hours later when the luggage was locked in the trunk, my wife and son were buckled into their seats, and I was ready to leave for the border, I forgot my instructions, turned the right-hand key first, and set off a shrill alarm which brought all the neighbors running.

In a sense, an alarm had been buzzing in my brain all summer. The car-rental agent hadn't exaggerated. As described by newspapers, magazines, and TV commentators, Italy was a country at war with itself. Economic and political collapse appeared imminent, inevitable. Premier Giulio Andreotti had formed a minority government which managed to keep the Christian Democrats in power, but only because the Communists and all other parties, except the neo-Fascist MSI, had agreed to abstain from parliamentary voting.

Enraged by this compromise and screaming of co-optation, far-left splinter groups, the *ultras*, called for struggle against "the system," of which communism was now an integral part. Daubing their faces with paint or donning masks, calling themselves Metropolitan Indians, anarchic gangs took to the streets, burning, looting, bombing, and shooting.

Loony as their appearance and actions were, the *ultras* could at least claim to be consistent. Viewing life through the prisms of Marxist propaganda, they believed they saw a classic scenario. Corruption, unemployment, and exploitation had, they thought, left Italy ripe for a takeover. But instead of helping them topple the Christian Democratic regime which had been in power since the end of World War II, the Communist party had chosen to prop it up. Having been offered the rope with which to hang capitalism, the Communists had timidly dropped their hands from the lever to the trap door and tiptoed down from the scaffold.

Clearly the Communists had no desire to take over during a crisis of such magnitude. What if they couldn't cope with it any better than the Christian Democrats had? People might start blaming them. And then where would they be? Although their reluctance was understandable—and although they could try to explain it away as patriotic cooperation—the Communists gave the logical lunatics no choice except violence.

The Fascists had long had no other choice or desire. Sometimes they fired back at the leftists; other times, it was rumored, they disguised themselves as leftists and fired first. Both extremist fringe groups claimed the Christian Democrats, and maybe the Communists, were involved in a conspiracy to provoke more violence so that the country would cry out for repression, even a dictatorship, anything to stop the disorder.

In America the media said the situation was reminiscent of Mussolini's rise to power, but the rhetoric and much of the film footage called to mind more recent events. One was reminded of our own urban riots—Watts, Newark, Detroit, Washington—and one could also imagine similarities to the cataclysms in Belfast or Beirut. In its cover article "Living with Anarchy" (August 1, 1977), *Newsweek* spoke of Italy's "vicious street crime, the wave of bloodshed," and illustrated the text with grisly photographs of dead and wounded bodies, armed guerrillas, and riot police wielding rifle butts. "The incidence of shootings and fire-bombings has grown out of all proportion," *Newsweek* claimed—and by not specifying "out of all proportion" to what, it let each reader substitute his most gruesome nightmares. Nobody mentioned that the incidence of violent crime, especially homicide, was five times higher in America, or that terrorists in Northern Ireland and Spain perpetrated far more assassinations than had the Red Brigades.

Although slightly more reserved, the *New York Times* ran stories about a Rome that had changed drastically and was now dirtier, more violent, sadder. *"La dolce vita* has become the dangerous life" (*NYT,* July 18). The *New Yorker* (May 2, 1977) reported that artists, directors, and the beautiful people huddled behind locked doors after dark, leaving the streets empty except for muggers and "nervous bachelors walking their new Dobermans."

Before I left for Rome, seldom a day went by that I didn't receive a letter from a relative or friend urging me not to go and telling me of one journalist or another who had been attacked by the Red Brigades, which had taken to ambushing newsmen. They aimed for the legs, shooting to cripple. Later on they started shooting to kill.

While I am not the sort of writer who can't resist a disaster or a war, I have often found myself wandering through countries which were in a state of crisis. Compared to trips I have made to Haiti, the Dominican Republic, Algeria, Morocco, Egypt, Israel, and Lebanon, Italy has always struck me as tame and pleasant, but this time I was uneasy—frightened, to tell the truth—especially about taking my family with me. Still, I had made up my mind to go and only in retrospect did I recognize how contradictory my reasons were.

On one hand, I had a novel to finish and an invitation

from the American Academy in Rome. Having lived in Italy
several times before, I was familiar with its faults and confu-
sions, but I like the people, the culture, the climate, the
food, and the pastimes which foreigners and natives alike
have enjoyed here for centuries. Say what you will about
New York, Paris, or London, for me nothing can compare
to walking through Rome, particularly on clear evenings
when the stones take on a warm, soft terra-cotta color.

On the other hand, I realized I was going to Italy out of
ghoulish curiosity, eager to study the country's deterioration
and try to understand what flaws in the national character
had brought on the current catastrophe. I also had an assignment from *Harper's Magazine* to write an article, the working title of which was "Life in the Ruins," and my eyes were
alert for signs of corruption, decay, and violence.

Historically, travelers to Italy have always had mixed
motives. Some came to conquer the country; others came to
yield to its charms. Some came to plunder; others were on
religious pilgrimages. Some saw it as a symbol of classical
refinement; others had visions of cheap wine and easy
women. Many claimed that only Italians knew how to live;
just as many believed Italians were incapable of running
their lives.

It didn't occur to me until later that my schizophrenic
reasons for moving to Italy were bound to split my percep-
tions into mutually exclusive categories. Nor did it dawn on
me that other writers—even the ones who had produced all
those scarifying articles I had read—were probably plagued
by contradictions similar to my own.

◆ ◆ ◆ ◆ ◆

It was a warm, bright day, the first Saturday in September,
when I drove east along the French Riviera, turned inland,
and took the autostrada into Italy. The changes were immediate and dramatic—but not the sort I had expected.

First, there was no bottleneck. After a few cursory questions and without a glance at our passports, the Italian guards waved us on. In the outbound lane, cars from all countries were waved through just as casually. Considering what I had read, I was surprised that the guards didn't search for weapons and dope going in, or fugitive terrorists and currency coming out—this latter indifference despite the fact that it was rumored that as much as fifty billion dollars of private capital had fled the country.

There was another notable fact. The last time I drove through this area, in April 1976, there hadn't been a single piece of loose change. At gas stations, restaurants, and toll-booths, if a customer didn't have the exact amount of lire, he was given postage stamps or hard candy instead of *spiccioli.*

Now there was still very little change, but a solution had been improvised. Private banks had printed their own currency in denominations of fifty and one hundred lire (six and twelve cents). Called *miniassegni,* these small bills were an open invitation to counterfeiters—I once got one with "Banca di Vermicelli" inscribed on it—and since they were run off on cheap paper, they couldn't be kept in circulation long.

The road was full of cars that day, roaring past at frightening speeds. I pushed the Fiat up to seventy-five miles per hour, and still they breezed by me, undaunted by any speed limit, by the long, twisting tunnels, or by the fact that gasoline cost two dollars and twenty cents a gallon.

They also seemed unaware that summer vacation was supposed to have ended. The coast was crowded, the Mediterranean aswarm with brown bodies, the resorts of Bordighera, San Remo, and Rapallo crawling with tourists—Italian tourists for the most part. Thus far, the country had kept its instability and deprivations well hidden.

Convinced I couldn't really see the country that was racing by on both sides of me, couldn't get a true feel for the place with a slab of concrete under me, I abandoned the autostrada near Pisa. But even up close, at ten miles per hour, things looked surprisingly placid. Although signs and scrawls of graffiti called for revolution, the only confrontations I saw were on narrow side streets where young boys played soccer; the only angry voices I heard were from the people who lived along the streets and were tired of having balls kicked against their doors and shutters.

◆ ◆ ◆ ◆ ◆

In the following days, as I hurried from town to town—San Gimignano, Siena, Arezzo, Cortona—I came as close to panic as I was ever to get in Italy. I now had less fear of being shot or swept up in a violent *manifestazione* than I did of being always in the wrong place at the wrong time. On the lookout for chaos, anarchy, and destruction, I saw antique furniture fairs, medieval pageants in elaborate costumes, religious festivals, and family picnics in bucolic settings which might have been lifted intact from frescoes by Giotto or Cimabue. Nervously prepared to defend my own small family, I found myself battling not with the Red Brigades or neo-Fascists, but with other mamas and papas, all of them smiling and muttering apologies, yet just as determined as I was to get a table in a restaurant, a room in a hotel.

It was both a relief and another disappointment then when we reached Cortona—a relief to have a reservation at Oasi, a monastery that had been converted into an elegant *albergo*, a disappointment to discover that the crisis-ridden Italy I had read about had once again eluded me. I was left with nothing to do except stroll through quiet olive groves, climb up to the walled city, tour the Etruscan ruins, and watch the sun give a perfect demonstration of chiaroscuro as it set behind the hills. After dinner and a bottle of wine we sadly returned to the room.

We had been in bed an hour when the bomb went off. The concussion nearly knocked us to the floor, and through the slats of the shutters we could see a raw phosphorescent glare. A second explosion rocked the stout monastery, rattling drain pipes. I crept close to the window and peered through the lattices, ready to risk almost anything to get my first glimpse of the action. Another spurt of flame arched over the valley and with a deafening thud it blossomed into a chrysanthemum of colors.

Fireworks! It was after midnight and somebody was shooting off fireworks in a blazing display that more than matched any American Fourth of July extravaganza. Angrily I flung open the shutters. The sky was as livid as I was, and I wondered what the hell they had to celebrate. Didn't they read the newspapers? Didn't they know or care what was happening to their country?

I sank down on the bedside and with no choice but to stay awake, I watched the display along with my wife and son, whose high spirits eventually routed my foul mood and helped put me in a frame of mind to realize my mistake. I had been looking in all the wrong places. *La dolce vita* would obviously last longer in coastal resorts and rural villages. If I meant to see, much less analyze, the country's plight, I had to plunge to the core of its urban corruption—that DMZ of deserted streets, bombed-out buildings, and deracinated survivors which journalists had breathlessly described.

Next morning I got back on the autostrada and raced toward Rome, stopping just long enough in Orvieto to eat lunch and watch a shapely teenage girl work on her forehand by whacking a tennis ball against a wall of the town's cathedral. No one else paid her any attention. I told myself it was because Italians feel more at ease with history and religion than do we Americans who have less of either.

But then on the way to the car I knew I'd have to rethink this relationship between Italians and religion. I had passed a billboard advertising blue jeans with the brand name of Jesus. The picture showed a woman's fleshy buttocks spilling out of denim shorts; the slogan read, "If you love me, follow me."

I had also noticed at each news kiosk one of the standard

features of secular democracy—hard-core pornography on open display. Supple as mink, couples, troikas, and four-somes copulated in positions that defied gravity and the imagination. Could the Catholic Church still be said to control this country?

There was no time to ponder the question. I pushed on toward Rome, where the real Italy started. Or where smug Milanese said that Africa started. A hundred miles farther south was Naples, the city which journalists called the Calcutta of Europe, and after that, the shabby foot of Italy's boot was, I had read, mired in the Third World.

◆ ◆ ◆ ◆ ◆

Driving into an Italian city for the first time is in many ways to discover the East, an oriental frame of mind with its resistance to straight lines and right angles. At bus stops, newsstands, bank windows, and public telephones people tend to form arabesques. The traffic, too, follows patterns seldom imagined north of the Alps. One-way streets suddenly switch directions. Or else they become two-way. Two-lane roads can be transformed into four-lane highways, sidewalks into exit ramps, alleys into cloverleafs. Red lights, stop signs, and pedestrian zones signify order only to the deluded or the soon to be dead.

In the course of ten blocks I was sideswiped by a weird three-wheeled vehicle called an Apecar, tried to catch the hit-and-run driver but got cut off by a VW bus full of nuns, and was stalled at an intersection where everybody had stopped to watch a fistfight. A boy on a motorbike had run into a couple in a car. After a ritual exchange of insults, the boy punched the man through the open window of the car. The man wanted to get out and fight, but his wife held him back. So he punched her—the best blow of the fracas—climbed out and wrestled the boy to the pavement.

By the time we reached our apartment I was trembling and soaked through with sweat and could well imagine that

9

many a visitor, even an experienced journalist, might spend an hour driving through Rome and decide that he had been caught up in the random antinomian violence of the city. But it was just another rush hour, and this seemed to me good preparation—a baptism of fire—for what I believed lay ahead.

◆ ◆ ◆ ◆ ◆

Leaving my wife and son locked in the apartment, I set off just after dark and walked toward Trastevere, an area which is invariably referred to in articles and tour guides as a workers' neighborhood. Narrow, twisting, and spooky with shadows, the streets leading down from the Janiculum Hill were eerily deserted, and I was tempted to turn back, call a taxi, and reconnoiter the combat zone from a fast-moving target. But then a few young people stepped out of the darkness and they were coming my way.

It was useless to try to outrun them uphill, so I plunged recklessly ahead, my breathing shallow and erratic. Maybe I looked menacing; perhaps I didn't appear rich enough to be worth mugging. Whatever their reasons, they made room for me and I hurried onto a broader, brightly lit street and stopped dead. I was surrounded.

Whole families strolled hand in hand. Mamas pushed baby carriages. Kids rode bikes or scooted along on skateboards. Leaning against trees, walls, and parked cars, lovers pressed together and kissed, oblivious to everybody. Piazza Santa Maria in Trastevere was packed. All the outdoor tables at Galeassi and Sabatini's were taken. The cafés and *gelaterie* were crowded, movie houses were mobbed, and pizzerias were steeped in customers and in the aroma of garlic and oregano. Haunch to haunch, an international brigade of hippies sat on the steps around the central fountain, talking, smoking, plucking guitars, and singing while German, American, and Japanese tour groups snapped pictures.

10

The flashbulbs reminded me of last night's fireworks and again I asked myself, more in bewilderment this time than in anger, what the hell was everybody celebrating? Didn't they know the rate of inflation, the unemployment figures, the enormity of the national debt, the dangers of being firebombed, shot in the kneecap, or knocked to the cobblestones by carabinieri?

Although I had a hard time believing it, this all looked remarkably like the Rome I had known for the last decade and I was tempted to conclude that these people, Italians and tourists alike, were reveling in the simple pleasures of being outdoors in the balmy night air, enjoying the delights of looking at street life which couldn't have been better choreographed.

Still I pressed on, full of gnawing uncertainties by now, yet expecting to see telltale signs of decline and imminent fall. Instead I saw boutiques named Twiggy and Ariel Unisex Casuals, and shops specializing in Scandinavian furniture, scented candles, and recycled jeans. No doubt there must have been a few workers who could afford to live in Trastevere, but a sign in English on one restaurant read, "Dine in a deconsecrated church. La Canonica offers you real Roman cooking right in the heart of Trestevere [sic]. Come 'n' get it." And two doors down from the Communist party headquarters stood the kind of knickknack shop one might see in Greenwich Village, Georgetown, or any American college town. It retailed Oriental lamps, rugs, brassware, leather goods, and jewelry. As Lenin might have expressed it, "You have nothing to lose except your slave bracelets."

♦ ♦ ♦ ♦ ♦

After that first night, even though I continued to do research for my article, "Life in the Ruins," I joined the celebration. It seemed impossible to live in Italy and not enjoy it. During the day I diligently tracked down officials to interview, studied news releases and reams of statistics about crime and

11

violence, and stalked the city for offbeat news items that might encapsulate the larger story, which everybody said was depressing.

Then in the evening, on tennis courts, in bars and restaurants, or at parties, I met other writers and journalists, and they all appeared to be in buoyant spirits. After a few drinks, they sometimes guiltily admitted that, in spite of everything, Italy was a terrific place to be. Many of them had lived here for years, had resigned positions or refused promotions that would have forced them to leave, and they hoped to stay on forever. Others returned over and over on assignments, brought their wives and families, and looked forward to visiting favorite cities and regions. Much as their stories might prophesy Armageddon, their assumption was that the country had a future which included them and their personal plans. It reminded me a bit of academics I had known in the late sixties and early seventies who were simultaneously predicting a revolution in America and buying and renovating colonial houses.

Of course journalists often have the freedom and professional detachment to have fun anywhere. So one should be hesitant about drawing conclusions. But it did seem that in 1977, no one was enjoying himself at the expense of the natives. Instead, as the unusually warm, dry autumn continued, one had a sense of sharing it with the Romans and the tourists who, despite the worldwide alarms on radio, TV, and in the newspapers, kept coming in record numbers.

Gradually this division between day and night, work and play, the grim, harshly lit picture of Italy in shambles and the romantic, gauzy image of the country after dark began to trouble me. I recalled my own contradictory reasons for being here and thought of the country's Janus face. It is a place people love, then hate themselves for loving. It attracts, then repels. As Luigi Barzini has written of so many hypocritical foreigners, "Of course, [they] could not help also seeing the gay, profane and corrupt reality, which was all around them. It did not disturb them. It shocked a few.

It seduced many. They enjoyed it. They had a wonderful time. But few would admit they had come principally for the fun of mingling with such contemptible people" *(The Italians)*.

I wound up wondering whether journalists don't sometimes take their hate and contempt out on Italy during the working day so that they can go on enjoying themselves after hours. For them, as for many novelists, the country serves as a sort of backdrop against which moral and political allegories can be played out in bold relief. Characters are depicted as searching here for perfection and beauty, knowledge or self-realization, but they usually end up disillusioned or dead. That's the moral of most of the fiction and the bottom line in much of the reporting.

Yet behind the backdrop, Italian life goes on, equally indifferent to the shape writers attempt to impose on it and to the object lessons they draw from it.

This is not to suggest that the country does not have serious troubles or that it isn't going through an extraordinarily difficult period in its history. I am simply pointing out that Italy's problems are neither unique nor unprecedented. For outsiders it may be consoling in the short run to think that the situation is the result of a particularly virulent brand of national corruption, inefficiency, and ineptitude. But the problems, it seems to me, are an early warning of what has become a worldwide phenomenon—the crisis brought on by inflated expectations, diminishing opportunities, finite resources, and changing values. Being marginally poorer and more fragile, Italy finds itself forced today to make adjustments which may confront other countries tomorrow.

Meanwhile the rest of us have the option of looking on from a disdainful distance, having decided in advance that Italy deserves whatever it gets. Or else we can come closer, regarding the country with the sympathy and interest it deserves, objective about its strengths as well as its weaknesses, and learning from both.

Predictions have become something of an international pastime, particularly after Aldo Moro's assassination. But in truth there is no way of guessing what will happen to Italy. Although it has faced sterner tests and survived, every country has a breaking point. Only one thing is certain. Whether Americans choose to laugh at it or learn from it, we should not delude ourselves that Italy's collapse—if it ever comes to that—will be the soundless fall of an old and noble tree in an isolated forest.

• • • • •

IS ANYBODY HOME?

Last May as I was packing my bags and preparing to leave America for the sixth time in eight years, I chanced to read an article by Edward Hoagland, "Do Writers Stay Home?" (*New York Times Book Review,* May 23, 1977), which gave me a moment's pause. Having just returned from Africa where he encountered few Americans and no writers, Hoagland decided that writers, especially young ones, do, indeed, stay home these days and he wondered what this signified. Was the nation's literature, like its politics, subsiding into isolationism? Had the ambiguities and agonies of the war in Vietnam left American authors limp and introspective? Shying away from larger responsibilities, ignoring the world outside, were they now self-absorbed, interested only in campaign reports from the sexual revolution? Whatever the answers, Hoagland clearly believed he had spotted a dangerous trend.

To be sure, the article caused me a measure of concern. Africa is, after all, a rather large piece of real estate, and I could not understand why Hoagland concluded he had the place to himself just because he had the good fortune not to bump into any other authors. Even if he didn't meet them, he should have known he wasn't the only writer on the road. Seldom a month goes by that some magazine doesn't run an article on Africa, the Middle East, Asia, or South America, and there has been no dearth of books from Americans about out-of-the-way places. At the time Hoagland was in the Sudan, for instance, William Harrison was in Kenya completing his excellent novel *Africana*, Eugene Linden had just published *The Alms Race*, an analysis of voluntary relief agencies in Lesotho, and Thurston Clarke was in Mali doing research for *The Last Caravan*, a definitive study of the 1973 drought in the Sahel.

I was also puzzled by Hoagland's short memory. Eighteen months earlier I had met him several times in Rome. On assignment for *Harper's*, he was headed for Israel, Egypt, and East Africa, and having never been to that part of the world before, he had stopped in London to see Paul Theroux and get names and addresses in East Africa. From me he got names and addresses in Egypt and Israel.

While we were both marking time until we departed—he for Cairo, I for Algeria—we kept running into other writers. Robert Penn Warren was in Italy finishing *A Place to Come To*, Norman Mailer was there doing a filmscript for Sergio Leone, and Donald Stewart, Robert Katz, and Gore Vidal, having lived in Rome for years, seemed to vie with one another in offering hospitality to junketing authors. It was a great surprise then when I heard Hoagland claim American writers were staying home.

◆ ◆ ◆ ◆ ◆

The magnitude of this surprise expanded exponentially when I returned to Europe this past year. Settling first in a small French village, I found myself surrounded by writers. In a neighboring hamlet William Wiser was finishing his novel *The Wolf Is Not Native to the South of France*, while in Cannes Harold Robbins was working diligently at his dictaphone, unspooling yet another best-seller. Gloria Emerson arrived to interview Graham Greene for *Rolling Stone,* and Douglas Day, whose biography of Malcolm Lowry won a National Book Award and whose novel *Journey of the Wolf* was set in Spain, passed through on his return from Madrid, where he had been covering the first elections since the Civil War.

In autumn, when I moved to Rome, the city was filled with American writers. William Murray was there to do an article for the *New Yorker* on the political situation. John Updike showed up for the Italian publication of *Marry Me.* Mary Lee Settle was in Umbria doing research for a new novel. (Her previous novel, *Blood Tie,* set in southern Turkey, had just won the National Book Award.) Prix de Rome–winning poet Daniel Epstein had taken up residence at the American Academy, but was on the road almost as often as he was in Rome. On a long trip through Africa, Epstein found he was following in the footsteps of another poet, Michael Harper, who had been arrested during a disturbance in Soweto. Then when Epstein returned to the American Academy, he discovered Peter Viereck had just left, that Anne Waldman, on her way to India, was in town for a few days, and that Kenneth Koch had settled in for a semester of teaching Italian junior high school students how to write poetry.

From listening to the literary grapevine, I knew James Merrill was in Athens, Philip Roth had been behind the Iron Curtain again, Paul Bowles and John Hopkins were, as usual, in Tangiers, William Humphrey had stopped in Paris, then went on to Scotland, and Ronald Sukenick had been in Montpellier, France, lecturing about the plight of the American writer. Having now given virtually the same lecture myself at three Italian universities, I have almost decided that the plight of the American writer is not that he has become a fretful, self-absorbed stay-at-home but rather that he is obsessed with seeing other countries and with the romantic idea that mere motion is a road to knowledge, a valid mode of perception, a smooth avenue to self-realization. Safer than heroin—although often just as expensive—travel is the contemporary artist's way of systematically deranging his senses. If Rimbaud were alive today, he would probably apply for an American Express Gold Card, wangle an assignment from a magazine, and set off to cover the war in the Horn of Africa.

More seriously, I believe American literature has little reason to fear that it is becoming too isolated and solipsistic, as Edward Hoagland seems to think, or that it is being damaged by foreign influences and frenetic travel, as I have jokingly suggested. The country is big enough, its culture diverse enough, to accommodate the broadest range of styles, interests, and sensibilities. While it is true that writers as different as Emily Dickinson and William Faulkner have demonstrated the advantages of staying close to home, it is also true that Herman Melville, Ernest Hemingway, Ezra Pound, Gore Vidal, and dozens of others have proved it doesn't necessarily hurt a novelist or poet to get around a little. If Walt Whitman gave good advice when he urged American writers to understand and appreciate their native ground, Henry James was no less wise when he showed that in some cases the best way to understand America—and oneself—is to leave it, at least for a while.

Of all the motives for taking off, perhaps too much has been made of those lofty goals of mastering a new language, meeting people, learning about another culture. Education is doubtless a noble aspiration, but not enough, in my opinion, has been said about the advantages of ignorance. Personally I would prefer to go places where at first I don't speak the language or know anybody, where I easily lose my direction and have no delusions that I'm in control. Feeling disoriented, even frightened, I find myself awake, alive, in ways I never would at home. All my senses suddenly alert, I can hear again, smell, see—and afterward, if I'm lucky, I can write.

Blank pages, blank spaces on a map, for me they are

much the same; I am anxious to get to the bottom of a mystery I am constantly in the process of formulating. Although neither urge is altogether explicable, I suspect why I write has a lot in common with why I travel, just as *how* I do both might best be expressed by a line from Theodore Roethke, "I learn by going where I have to go."

◆ ◆ ◆ ◆ ◆

EL OUED

Men may climb mountains just because they are there, but most travelers require more of a destination than the simple fact of its existence. When I first set out for Algeria, I thought I had ample reasons. Although I had been to the Sahara before, skirting its western rim in Morocco and its eastern edges in Egypt, I wanted to see the Grand Oriental Erg, an area of sand dunes sculpted by wind into wavelike crests several hundred feet high.

I was also eager to visit El Oued, a desert station whose architecture is as distinctive as the surrounding countryside. Viewed from a low-flying airplane, the town resembles a clump of beehives. Often called "the city of a thousand cupolas," El Oued is constructed out of hand-molded mud, and every building, even the smallest hut, is roofed by domes and barrel vaults that keep the interiors cool.

In the ocean of sand that encircles the city, there is an archipelago of oases, some of which sprout only a handful of palm trees and bear an uncanny resemblance to the desert islands one sees in cartoons. Because the dunes move with

20

the wind and frequently flood the oases, farmers have to fight back the Sahara with buckets and shovels. Every day they dig out the dust that has accumulated in their fields during the night, then pile it at the periphery of the arable land, where it mounts up like the sand in an hourglass. The palm trees now stand in hollows fifty and sixty feet deep, their roots straining for buried moisture, their fronds barely visible above ground level. Nurtured and protected with enormous effort, the dates of this region are reputed to be the most delicious in Africa.

El Oued intrigued me most, however, because it had once been the home of Isabelle Eberhardt. The illegitimate daughter of an exiled Russian anarchist, she seemed to require a vast stage for her theatrical personality—and what proscenium could be wider and more melodramatic than the Sahara? Arriving in 1899 at the age of twenty-two, Eberhardt promptly set about scandalizing the natives and the French colonists alike. Born Jewish, she converted to Islam and married an Algerian, then dressed as an Arab man, referred to herself as Si Mahmoud, and joined a camel caravan. Eventually she fell in with the Foreign Legion, entertaining them with Russian songs while accompanying herself on the piano and generally "sleeping her way through the *Armée d'Afrique,*" as one historian put it. As fate and her nature might have decreed, she met a bizarre end. In one of the world's most arid regions, she died in a flash flood.

If all this esoteric lore weren't enough to entice me, El Oued had a new attraction—the Souf Museum. When I went to the Algerian Embassy in Rome to pick up my visa, the officials there described it as a rich repository of desert flora and fauna, of native art and local handicrafts. Caught up in their own enthusiasm, they couldn't concentrate on my mundane questions about itineraries. When I told them I intended to fly to Tunis, rent a car, and drive south, crossing the border near Nefta, they nodded absentmindedly and continued extolling the marvels of the Souf Museum.

21

In Tunis, the Avis agent wasn't much more attentive. When I explained where I planned to go, he said, *"Ça va,"* and returned to his glass of mint tea.

By that afternoon, I had reached the desert and was driving across a dry lake bed, its surface baked hard and bleached by the sun. In southern Tunisia, all the towns seemed to boast monumental arched entrances that led down a long desolate modern boulevard named after the day a holy man had been martyred or a revolution had started. Out the corner of my eye, I caught flickering glimpses, like pictures on a video tape in fast forward, of camels in courtyards, artisans pounding brass trays, veiled women balancing earthen jars on their heads.

By the time I got to Tozeur, it was growing dark and the frantic life of the side streets had spilled out onto the main thoroughfare. People in flowing robes flapped like giant bats across the road, paying no heed to the traffic. I was caught behind a man who pushed a cart piled high with round loaves of bread as big as sewer lids. In the other lane, striding toward me, were two bearded gentlemen holding hands. One had a live sheep saddled over his shoulders; the other carried a goatskin water bag. Crowds of kids trotted along beside my car, rapping their knuckles against the door panels, offering to be my guide, asking for cigarettes and spare change. Directly behind me, bearing down hard, was a bus labeled SPIES in giant red letters. SPIES—pronounced "speece"—was a Danish tour group, but I couldn't help feeling I was under the combined scrutiny of the CIA and KGB.

To add to the eeriness of my arrival in Tozeur, my hotel had been taken over by a contingent of midgets. George Lucas was in town shooting a *Star Wars* sequel, and the little people had been imported to play androids and Ewoks. The hotel manager shunted me off to a caravansary that looked as if it had been constructed by, and might still be inhabited by, mud daubers. Still, everybody was extremely polite and overwhelmed me with friendship. They also professed to

envy me my trip to El Oued where, they said, I must be sure
to visit the Souf Museum, which had started to assume in
my mind the magnificence of the Louvre or the Metropolitan.

In the morning, I woke to the cry of the muezzin. Or
rather to a scratchy recording of a muezzin broadcast over
a loudspeaker. In the courtyard, next to a pond covered with
green scum so thick I could have scribbled my name in it,
I was served a breakfast of café au lait and mud balls.
Following the example of other guests, I whacked a mud ball
with a spoon, knocked off the crust of dirt, and found an
orange underneath. I peeled it and ate it with no ill effects.
In fact, I felt quite exuberant at how close I was to my
destination.

My exuberance lasted less than two hours, just the time
it took to pass through Nefta and on to the Algerian border,
where authorities said I could cross, but insisted the car had
to stay behind. It didn't matter what I thought I had been
told by the embassy in Rome or the Avis agent in Tunis. I
didn't have the correct documents or the proper insurance
to bring a rental car into Algeria.

Returning to Nefta, I considered my alternatives. It struck
me as intolerable to travel this far—no more than a short
drive from the Grand Oriental Erg and the fabled Souf
Museum—only to fall frustratingly short. I wondered what
Isabelle Eberhardt would have done. Surely she wouldn't
have let petty restrictions ruin an adventure. She would have
gone native and gotten through. I decided to do the same.

Throughout the Sahara, there exists a long-distance taxi
service that connects towns. The contemporary equivalent of
a camel caravan, it consists of private cars called *louages*
which trundle across the desert, dropping passengers along
the way. They have no fixed schedules or set fees. You
simply go to some central point—usually the market—find
a driver who is headed in your direction, haggle over a price,
then wait while he collars enough customers to fill his car.

The *louage* from Nefta to El Oued was an ancient Peugeot

whose hood, fenders, and grille had been smeared with grease to prevent blowing sand from eating away the metal. A brass Hand of Fatima dangled from the rearview mirror as an amulet to ward off the evil eye. Once we were rolling, I realized how desperately we needed this good-luck charm. The driver had a relaxed, loose-wristed style, and as he barreled toward the border at eighty miles an hour, he kept one hand on the horn and the other on the radio dial. He was quite adept at steering with his knees and he depended on instinct and swift reflexes as he rounded curves, hogging the middle of the road. If anybody had been headed our way, we would have been reduced to hamburger. Other *louages* had already gone through the grinder, and the roadside was strewn with their scorched and gutted remains.

After a pause at customs control, we pushed on into Algeria, and it seemed that all the sand had been blown out of Tunisia and had piled up on this side of the frontier. Soon we were deep in dunes that crowded the road, sometimes reducing it to a single tortuous lane, sometimes covering the asphalt in drifts which we had to detour around. Even with the windows closed, I could hear dust buzzing at the glass and I could taste grit in the air.

From time to time, kids came running out of the dunes, dancing in front of the hurtling *louage*, holding up sand roses, amethysts, and handicrafts they hoped to sell. But the driver plowed on through. He stopped just once to let off a passenger who was lugging two large raffia baskets full of croissants and baguettes of bread. The fellow marched straight up a dune toward nothing I could see. He might have been a character trudging through a landscape conjured up by Beckett or Ionesco. Then again, maybe he meant to open a bakery at the crest of the dune.

Farther on, we happened upon another surrealistic scene. A shovel brigade was working to clear the road, but it was a Sisyphean task. No matter where they dumped the sand, it drifted back onto the asphalt. Long white snakes of it slithered ahead of the *louage*, leading us down a boulevard lined by palm trees and oleander bushes which the wind was lashing left and right. At last, we had arrived in El Oued, and I could not have been more relieved and grateful had I come by camel, surviving an overland trek from Timbuktu.

"The city of a thousand cupolas" proved to be that rare destination, a place which delivered almost exactly what I had imagined. There were no tour groups and few foreigners. The local citizens had little interest in outsiders and even less in serving as guides or gofers. In fact, they seemed as hard and austere as the land in which they lived. Even the shopkeepers in the bazaar were solemn-faced and much too dignified to hawk their wares or bargain over prices. While this might make El Oued sound grim and inhospitable, it was actually one of the most pleasant towns I have visited in the Arab world. Free of the hands-on, full-court press of touts and hustlers, blessedly relieved of the oleaginous charms of those polyglot, omnipresent guides who do so much to misdirect visitors in other cities, I found I could go anywhere and never be bothered. I could pause and look around without fear of being trapped in an octopoid embrace by somebody babbling, "Welcome, I am your friend. Speak Englees. Come to my shop."

Needless to say, I didn't miss the Souf Museum. It was the high point of my trip, although not entirely in the manner I had been led to expect. At first, upon entering it, I thought there had been a mistake. No larger than a three-car garage, it looked like the cluttered storeroom of an aging eccentric. Just inside the door stood what appeared to be the business end of a feather duster. According to a label, it was the last ostrich seen in this part of the Sahara. A French Legionnaire had shot it in 1937.

There were some carpets and antique jewels, wall maps and enlarged photographs of the oases. But the bulk of the exhibit—or at least what had the most dramatic impact on me—was an ambitious collection of venomous snakes the size of earthworms, intestinal worms the size of boa constrictors, scorpions the size of ten-dollar lobsters, horned beetles as big as Princess telephones, hairy spiders, bristling lizards, and blood-sucking centipedes.

The prizewinner, however, was a wineglass filled with formaldehyde in which fat gray blobs floated around like rotten grapes. I suppose the indigenous populace had no trouble making sense of this display, but for out-of-towners there was a thoughtful typewritten card in three languages which identified it as "Blood-Engorged Ticks."

◆ ◆ ◆ ◆ ◆

THE GREAT RAILWAY BAZAAR: BY TRAIN THROUGH ASIA*

Some writers take to drink, some to drugs. Others with the requisite energy delve into sex, straight or deviate. The heartiest—or perhaps the most foolhardy—try traveling. At times it's an excuse to escape working, but just as often it's an attempt to outflank the abominable blank page and come at it from an oblique angle. The point, as Graham Greene put it in his autobiography, *A Sort of Life,* is to engage the menace of boredom in a battle to the death.

Paul Theroux, a thirty-three-year-old novelist with eight books to his credit, seemed to have had something like this in mind when he set out from London on the Orient Express and kept on going—via the Khyber Pass Local, the Frontier Mail, the Golden Arrow to Kuala Lumpur, the Mandalay Express, the Ozora Limited—until he got to Tokyo and turned around to board the Trans-Siberian Express for England. In his words, "I felt flayed by the four months of train

*A review of *The Great Railway Bazaar: By Train Through Asia* by Paul Theroux.

27

travel; it was as if I had undergone some harrowing cure, sickening myself on my addiction in order to be free of it."

Although aware of the eccentricity, the dizzying purpose-lessness, of the parabola he describes across one whole hemisphere, Mr. Theroux realizes he was simultaneously experiencing another trip. "Train travel animated my imagi-nation and usually gave me the solitude to order and write my thoughts: I traveled easily in two directions, along the level rails while Asia flashed changes at the window, and at the interior rim of a private world of memory and language."

For the reader the rewards of *The Great Railway Bazaar* come on different levels too. On the surface there are the delights produced by intriguing people and exotic places. Annoying though they probably were to the author at the time, the other passengers spill through these pages with the kind of gaudy variety and verve which a fiction writer would love to create out of whole cloth. Aspiring prophets from California on their way to ashrams in India, smugglers of opium and armaments, drug addicts and derelicts seeking anonymity in the East, Texas oil workers on a binge in Tehran, American Embassy employees who seem to do little except discuss the state of their bowels, an Afghan tribes-man who fires his shotgun through the roof of a bus, direc-tors of Vietnam tourism determined to turn the country into a resort once the guns are silent, pimps who purvey a sexual menu which would bugger . . . correction, beggar the imagi-nation. These characters and dozens more flesh out what could have been a tedious travelogue.

But the chief delight of this book is the insight it offers into Mr. Theroux's quick, witty, and quirky mind. Though merciless in his judgments and opinions, he usually has the saving grace of good humor and self-deprecation. While delivering a lecture on American literature in famine-stricken Ceylon, he can't understand how he managed to attract such a large audience . . . until lunch is served and he realizes the people have come for the free food.

An army, it is said, travels on its stomach. The finest writers, it seems, skim along on all five senses. Certainly Theroux's eyes are always open for a telling detail. In Vietnam the railroad bridges and gulleys beneath them become a metaphor for the long, tangled war. "Some rivers contained masses of broken bridges, black knots of steel bunched grotesquely at the level of the water. They were not all recent. In the gorges where there were two or three, I took the oldest ones to be relics of Japanese bombing, and others to be examples of demolition from the later terrorism of the fifties and sixties, each war leaving its own unique wreck. They were impressively mangled, like outrageous metal sculptures. The Vietnamese hung their washing on them."

Throughout Asia, enormous ironies appear to rise naturally from the landscape, but it takes an author of Theroux's intelligence and verbal gifts to capture them. "Burma is a socialist country with a notorious bureaucracy. But it is a bureaucracy that is Buddhist in nature, for not only is it necessary to be a Buddhist in order to tolerate it, but the Burmese bureaucratic delays are a consistent encouragement to a kind of traditional piety—the commissar and the monk meeting as equals on the common ground of indolent and smiling unhelpfulness."

Even Theroux's olfactory senses serve him well. "As Calcutta smells of death and Bombay of money, Bangkok smells of sex, but this sexual aroma is mingled with the sharper whiffs of death and money."

Theroux's genius for the incisive and amusing generalization tempts him occasionally to overstep his knowledge and understanding of a particular place or people. The result is sometimes an unfortunate arch tone and a prose, reeking of racism and xenophobia, that could have been cribbed from Kipling. "The food [in Afghanistan] smells of cholera, travel there is always uncomfortable and sometimes dangerous, and the Afghans are lazy, idle, and violent."

I prefer to regard such passages as momentary failures of imagination rather than as flaws of character. For it seems to me a reader with an urge for a trip in entertaining and intelligent company could scarcely do better than to board *The Great Railway Bazaar* with Paul Theroux and stay put until the last station.

♦ ♦ ♦ ♦ ♦

FROM EQUINOX TO SOLSTICE
AND BEYOND

Autumn in Italy is a season measured by climate rather than the calendar. *Ottobrata romana,* a string of crisp mornings and balmy afternoons, can be literally translated as "Roman October," but it is not limited to a single month any more than its glazed light, intense colors, and vivacious mood can be captured in a single word. With luck, the warm, sunny days stretch well into November, even December, and when the wind blows from the south, out of Africa, the air is heavy with heat and crackling with static electricity. One sees then on back streets the familiar rituals of summer reenacted. Housewives water down the cobblestones in front of their buildings and hang carpets over windowsills and wallop away the grit of the Sahara.

During a Roman fall, there is rarely a frost and the trees don't flame with extravagant colors. The most dramatic change is in the sky, in the depth and quality of the light, the play of shadows on the city's convoluted spaces, which are as chambered and complex as a nautilus shell. Mist rises from the Tiber on most mornings; the sun burns without focus until it achieves its milky apogee at noon; then as evening advances the sky takes on the clarity of *vino bianco.*

Although the dying leaves don't have the brilliance of American elms, maples, and oaks, Rome in autumn doesn't lack color. In fact, one sees everywhere radiant shades of orange, red, and purple that would rival any New England forest. But these colors appear on the buildings and ruins, not in the vegetation. Vistas that appeared washed out and flat during August now seem to burn with smokeless fire.

Flamboyant color is also plentiful in the city's flower markets, particularly Campo dei Fiori, and as November first approaches, chrysanthemums as big as cabbages are sold on almost every street corner. Chrysanthemums always remind me of college football games and the corsages coeds wear on their coats. But for Italians they carry altogether different memories. I once made the mistake of buying a chrysanthemum and bringing it as a gift to the hostess of a large dinner party. The reactions of the other guests ranged from perplexed to appalled. After an awkward pause, the hostess explained that a chrysanthemum is a flower for the dead, the centerpiece of the kind of bouquet an Italian puts on his mother's grave for All Souls' Day.

The smell of fall in Rome is much the same as that of autumn in America—the smell of melancholy, loss, and memory, of roasting chestnuts, wood smoke, and burning leaves. But there is also the aroma of food, for the older the season grows and the sooner the weather is apt to change and chase everybody indoors, the more urgent it is to eat a last meal al fresco. So the streets are crowded and redolent of garlic and oregano, clam sauce and pizza crust, Gorgonzola and *funghi porcini.*

At Dal Bolognese on Piazza del Popolo, I once saw a party of eight pass around a truffle the size of a man's fist. Each person sniffed it, then shut his eyes in ecstasy as if savoring the scent of a Roman autumn. They handed it back to the waiter and let him shave slices onto their pasta.

Smelling, tasting, looking, feeling—everybody during

this season seems to be storing up sensations and memories as a defense against what they know is coming. Eventually, the weather will break with all the abrupt emphasis of a slamming door and cold rain will soak the city.

If the streets are the Romans' real home, then during these first wet, chill days, the city has the haunted look of a home abandoned. Grass sprouts in the cracks between cobblestones, and white marble slabs become veined with green moss. Metal flanges and bolts that help hold together the classical antiquities bleed rust. A vast loneliness settles over the city, and nothing is more forlorn than the empty piazzas where puddles swell slowly into lakes, and tables and chairs are stacked haphazardly outside of cafés like jetsam tossed up by high tide.

Afterward, the season is still autumn, but when the sun reappears, it is too feeble to offer the same warmth, too wan to deepen Rome's pastels. Dead leaves and pine needles mat the streets, temporarily hushing the traffic, and pedestrians congregate in amazement on bridges, gaping down at the Tiber, which splashes in whitecaps over the quays.

When the temperature drops still further, it is not uncommon for snow to fall outside the city in the Castelli Romani, the hills rising behind Frascati. The best indication that the thermometer in Rome hovers around the freezing mark is when housewives in poorer neighborhoods begin putting perishable food outside on window ledges and elsewhere. One icy December morning, I walked down a narrow street under a clotheslines where, next to trousers and socks, two filets of veal, pale as underpants, had been pinned to the wire to keep them fresh for dinner.

Not so long ago, it was common for Italians to exchange gifts on January 6, the Feast of the Nativity, not December 25. And children went to bed wondering whether Befana, a witch, not a jolly Santa Claus, would bring presents or chunks of coal. But, as in many corners of the globe, the Anglo-American concept of Christmas has made deep inroads here. Fir trees, turkeys, holly, and Santa Claus, once notions confined to the north, have invaded Rome. On the shopping streets of Via Condotti, Via Borgognona, and Via Frattina, the seasonal hallmarks are the same as those on Fifth Avenue, Rue de Faubourg St. Honoré, or Old Bond Street. There are flickering lights, tinsel-strewn trees, and pictures of Santa's rosy, smiling mug that might have been lifted from a Coca-Cola commercial. At the same time, there are bagpipe players down from the mountain reaches of the Abruzzi, blowing baleful skirling tunes, dressed in leather leggings, sheepskin vests, and slouch hats. Romans regard the players as a joyous sign that Christmas is near.

There are other signs of clashing traditions, some obvious, some subtle. At one end of the outdoor market on Campo dei Fiori, the flower vendors for whom the square is named begin to sell mistletoe, holly, pine trees, and pots of blazing poinsettias. At the other end of the market, which smells perpetually of seafood, hundreds of eels writhe in plastic basins, some of the slippery creatures the size of fingers, others as long and as fat as a man's arm. Although many Italians serve turkey on Christmas day, the Roman tradition is to eat eels the night before.

Even such a familiar seasonal symbol as holly is not without surprises. Our first Christmas in Rome, my wife bought a beautiful wreath that had gleaming green leaves and red berries that looked large and luscious enough to eat. This, we thought, was holly that would have been the pride of a horticulturist, a hybrid of the very best seeds.

It took our cleaning woman ten seconds to puncture our illusions. She told us almost all the holly in Rome is fake, a kind of confection cobbled together for homesick foreigners. When I protested that the leaves and berries on our wreath not only looked real, but felt real, she urged me to take a closer look and gave me a hint by flicking one fat berry with her fingernail.

At last I saw what she meant. Both the prickly leaves and shiny berries were indeed genuine, but they hadn't grown on the same bush. With an effort and a meticulousness that were unimaginable to me, somebody had plucked the berries from one type of bush, then fastened them with thin wire to sprigs of leaves from an altogether different bush. Not a single berry was out of place, and, unless one nudged aside the leaves, not a centimeter of wire was visible.

I suppose there are some who might complain that this mass marketing of fake holly is a kind of fraud. But it seems to me to represent all that is best about Italians—the desire to give people what they want, the determination to make the most of what they have, and the skill and imagination to create a convincing trompe l'oeil.

Whatever else has changed, one seasonal assumption has remained the same and is expressed in an often heard aphorism: *Natale con i tuoi, Pasqua con chi vuoi;* Christmas with your family, Easter with whomever you like.

For those who have families, and more important, families they love, this is scarcely a difficult stricture. But despite Italy's warmth and hospitality at other times, during this season the country can be hard on strangers, on the lonely, and on tourists just passing through. On Christmas Eve and the following day, shops are closed, as are most restaurants and movies. Buses don't run and taxis are rare. Local newspapers don't go to press and foreign ones are impossible to find. What's worse, the same thing happens again on New Year's Eve.

But at least on New Year's Eve there are the consolations of quirky drama. At midnight, the city explodes as Romans hurl firecrackers and old crockery out their windows. At the first light of dawn, those who have guts and immunity to microbes strip off their clothes and dive from bridges into the Tiber, washing away the past, readying themselves for the future.

◆ ◆ ◆ ◆ ◆

GETTING PLUGGED IN

In the United States it is commonplace to observe that the neighborhood—or indeed the entire town—where one grew up has changed beyond recognition. Either the old homestead has been razed to make room for a gas station or shopping center, or it has been tarted up—gentrified, as they say—and turned into a boutique. As millions of acres of countryside and cityscape have disappeared beneath asphalt and office buildings, former inhabitants feel a bit like amnesia victims.

Since World War II, Europe has undergone something of the same disorienting transformation. A number of cities—Berlin, Rotterdam, large parts of London—were bombed to rubble and had to be rebuilt from the ground up. But few urban planners were satisfied to recreate the original skylines. Instead, they seemed dead set on imitating New York City, and they put up buildings that resemble file cabinets and rocket ships.

In the past decades, even cities untouched by battle have changed. In Paris, high rises now loom behind famous horizons. A clutch of skyscrapers called La Défense defiles the view of the Arc de Triomphe. The shores of the Seine were once the quiet preserve of young impetuous lovers and old patient fishermen; today they reverberate with the thunderous racket of the Indianapolis 500, since roads have been widened to four-lane highways loud enough to frighten fish and daunt all but the most ardent lovers.

Among European capitals only Rome remains essentially the same. Although its population has doubled in the last forty years, the city retains the distinction of being less an urban center than a constellation of small villages, each with its own churches, shops, fountains, and restaurants.

True, Rome has traffic to rival any large city's. But it rumbles along—and frequently stalls—on roads that haven't changed much in centuries. Although Mussolini did broaden and straighten several major arteries, many streets are still the size of footpaths, and some are paved with teeth-rattling, chassis-destroying stones. Whether seen from a sixteenth-century carriage on the Pincian Hill or a twentieth-century motor scooter on the Janiculum Hill, the skyline is a consolation for those disconcerted by life's flux. There are the same majestic domes and cupolas and red brick ruins, the same serene flocks of swifts wheeling against the sky. At a distance, even the frothy white confection of the Vittorio Emmanuele monument, built in the nineteenth century, looks classical, timeless. Few new buildings rise in the *centro storico*. And none exceeds the height of St. Peter's.

Down off the hills, Rome is hardly an untouched enclave of historical sites and folkloric scenes of aged ladies in black setting out plates of pasta for stray cats. There are the usual signs of Coca-colonization. Walk a block in any direction and you'll bump into snack bars and discount outlets specializing in recycled blue jeans and punk jewelry. In Trastevere, supposedly the most typical Roman neighborhood, you'll pass a barbershop called Hippy Hairstyles and a store that advertises hand-tooled Texas cowboy boots. But unlike in London, Paris, Amsterdam, Bonn, Madrid, and Athens, you

37

will find no franchise hamburger chains,* no Kentucky Fried Chicken, no International Pancake House, no shopping center, no drive-ins, no section of the city that is crowded with workers during the day only to be deserted at night.

Although this sounds close to idyllic, there are disadvantages to living in a place that has remained the same for centuries. Last year Andrea Lee, a young American novelist and *New Yorker* staff writer, pinpointed several of these drawbacks in an interview with the *Washington Post*. Having moved here two years ago with her husband, an investment banker, Lee told the *Post*, "Rome's a beautiful city, but it's a terrible backwater. Very provincial. I miss decent films, art and photographic exhibitions, theater. I can't wait to get out of here. I'm dying to go to Paris where some twentieth-century things are happening."

Lee's remarks caused resentment, not just in the expatriate community, which tends to be touchy about its adopted home, but also among native Romans, who are normally indifferent to the opinions of foreigners. Yet while one could quibble over this point or that, Lee's remarks were generally on target. Rome's museums contain marvelous collections of antiquities, but they offer little modern art. And it's not simply that Rome doesn't measure up to other European capitals; it is often second-rate even within Italy. In opera and ballet, it can't compare with Milan. Florence often stages more and better concerts, and Venice has its International Film Festival and Biennale exhibitions. Touring shows of painting and sculpture tend to make a circuit of the lucrative markets in the north, rarely traveling south.

Rome has its share of movie houses, but most feature schlock produced strictly for domestic consumption or worse schlock imported from America and dubbed in Italian. Unlike London and Paris, where cinemas showcase current

---

*Read "The Junk Food Wars" to see how times and Rome have changed in two years.

38

foreign movies, old favorites, and classics, Rome has just one English-language movie house, the Pasquino, which seldom screens a film less than a year old, always reruns it until the print turns transparent with age, and occasionally projects the reels out of order.

Life here can provoke acute withdrawal symptoms in Americans accustomed to information overload in the United States. Especially for newspaper junkies who have yet to master Italian, this city is strictly cold turkey. The thin *International Herald Tribune,* more than half of its pages given over to ads and economic reports, is home-delivered at dawn in France, England, and Germany. But it straggles into Rome like a sleepy bureaucrat returning from a two-pasta lunch and makes it to selected kiosks by midafternoon with two-day-old news.*

That's better, though, than the *New York Times,* which never arrives at all. In other European capitals, one can always track down the Sunday *Times,* pay an exorbitant sum, and indulge in a media massage guaranteed to cure homesickness. But in Rome, even the *Times* bureau chief doesn't receive copies until they are weeks out of date.

These deprivations pale in significance, however, compared to the trauma that struck last summer. Bruce Springsteen announced that Italy would be included on his European tour, but he performed in Milan, not Rome. It was another insult to the Eternal City, another reminder that, whereas most urban areas are obsessed with seasonal fads, the trend of the month, and the restaurant or nightclub of the week, the calendar in Rome seems to register nothing except decades. The past matters more here, it would seem, than the present.

But one facet of Roman life is utterly contemporary and completely plugged into the feverish pulse of the rest of the world: Italian television. By any measure, even by American

---

*Finally, in June 1987, the *Trib* opened a printing plant in Rome and can now be bought in the morning.

standards, it's an up-to-date, state-of-the-art operation. To appreciate just how privileged Italian TV viewers are, one must understand something about TV elsewhere in Europe. For the most part, it is a state monopoly and, on both sides of the Iron Curtain, it is regarded as a crude political tool. Programming starts late in the day—in England the advent of morning news in 1983 was regarded as a revolutionary event—and goes off at midnight or earlier. Worse, it is limited to three or four channels, which cautiously support the party in power, give short shrift to opposing points of view, and often air boring programs.

German TV favors chunky yodelers in dirndls and lederhosen. An evening's entertainment on Spanish television is apt to be a military band playing marching tunes. The French are inclined to broadcast forty-year-old Jerry Lewis films, followed by hours of earnest debate by bearded *cinéastes*. Although BBC has earned high praise for its adaptation of literary classics and a number of truly funny situation comedies, which have even been exported to the United States, much of its programming consists of discussions of compost heaps and the problems of housebreaking a corgi.

In contrast, the television in my Roman apartment has no outside antenna, no cable, no special adapters, yet it brings in over fifty channels, including Antenne II from Paris and TV Monte Carlo from Monaco. Many stations stay on around the clock, competing for viewers with shows that range from highbrow to lowbrow to lobotomized.

The most popular programs originate in Milan on Canale 5, Rete Quattro, and Italia Uno, a triad of channels owned by Silvio Berlusconi, an enterprising fellow who developed a national network from a regional base for the first time in Italy. Several years ago, when the government took its first tentative steps toward deregulating television, it decreed that RAI (the government-owned network) would retain its national monopoly but that local stations were free to broadcast whatever and whenever they wanted. Berlusconi promptly set up local stations throughout the country and, although he could not send signals to his affiliates over the air or by satellite, he hired a team of motorcycle deliverymen to speed tapes from home base in Milan to the far reaches of the peninsula every day.

Admittedly, much of the programming on Berlusconi's video empire and competing channels is the sort of drivel one wouldn't dream of watching. There are daytime soap operas from America and Brazil, the nightly glitz of "Dallas," "Dynasty," "Falcon Crest," and dozens of their clones, and soft-core porn from Sweden and Turkey.

But there is also an impressive schedule of ballet, opera, concerts (including performances by Van Karajan and Bernstein at the Vatican), and drama ranging from Shakespeare to Pirandello. There are pungent satires from all points on the political spectrum, risqué variety shows that rival any in Paris or Las Vegas, the best specials from CBS, NBC, and ABC, and the cream of the crop from other European countries. In addition to new movies, there are frequent retrospectives of work by directors such as Fellini, Visconti, and Bergman, and by actors like Charlie Chaplin, Humphrey Bogart, and Nino Manfredi. The kinds of events one sees in the States only on pay TV—jazz festivals, rock concerts, MTV, and sports from USA and ESPN cable networks—are available in Rome for free. Despite the long shadow of the Vatican, there are even fundamentalist preachers filling the airways at odd hours. Watching Herbert Armstrong nattering away, in English, no less, about Armageddon, one cannot help wondering whether Rome is a lot less eternal than advertised.

But in January a different sort of drama absorbs me and most Americans living in Rome. As we follow the televised NFL play-off games and make plans for a dinner party during the Super Bowl, all sense of isolation and homesickness slips away. Convinced I'm a citizen of a global village,

41

I feel a rush of affection for my home country. But I believe it's better to sample the crackling high voltage of the States in small doses, through a cathode-ray tube. The messages reach me in a vague way, like a piece of music overheard in the street, all the more appealing for being half-remembered, half-imagined.

A CLEAN WELL-LIGHTED
PLACE . . . SORT OF

In March, after weeks of pelting rain, Rome experiences half a dozen mild spells, interspersed with cold snaps, before spring truly arrives. But with every warm wind, every bright day when the sky seems to have been scoured and the sun blinks back from windows, people stumble into the streets, pale and groggy as animals jolted out of hibernation. Immediately they start foraging. What they are searching for is not food; it is some indisputable proof that the season has changed for good.

Since Rome has less green space and fewer parks than any major city in Europe, these searchers are forced to adjust their sights and keep a sharp eye out for tiny flowers blooming in the Aurelian wall, yellow splashes of forsythia and mimosa spilling over the railings of rooftop terraces, wisteria vines climbing the walls of private courtyards. The most blatant evidence, however, is all around them. Outdoor cafés are full again, and lazy bees drone above the sugar bowls, as sure a sign of spring in Rome as the return of robins in the United States.

Suddenly the city resembles an al fresco session of the United Nations. Japanese emblazoned with Gucci labels take their tables. Delegates from the Arab Emirates sit sipping strong coffee and reading newspapers that have elegant blue and red characters. Coatless Germans and Scandinavians, their arms bare, their shirts unbuttoned, lean back in their chairs, convinced this is sunbathing weather. Italians are easily identifiable; many of them hold in their laps the radios they have prudently unscrewed from the dashboards of their cars to thwart thieves.

At the sight of crowded cafés, I am always reminded of my maiden voyage to Europe. In 1968, I sailed for France with my imagination addled by years of reading about Paris in the twenties, about expatriate authors settling in at the Dôme or the Select or La Closerie des Lilas to write the Great American Novel.

Not that I deluded myself that I would become the Hemingway of my generation or even that I wanted to set up shop in the literary haunts of Montparnasse. It was just that I felt sure I would find "my" café, my own Clean Well-Lighted Place, and would write there well and true, as Papa might have put it.

It didn't work out that way. Not in Paris. Not on the Riviera, not in London or Marbella or Granada or Marrakech or Athens or Cairo—all places in which I later spent long stretches of time writing. Everywhere I went, the cafés were too crowded, too chaotic, too costly, too cold, too cacophonous. Jukeboxes blared, waiters called out orders, and tourists nattered about airline connections and intestinal disorders. Kids played pinball machines and video games, and I had a hard time concentrating on football scores in the *International Herald Tribune,* much less following James Joyce's example and "forging in the smithy of my soul the uncreated conscience of my race."

In the past eighteen years I have traveled throughout Europe, North Africa, and the Middle East and have witnessed many wonders in cafés. I've seen a two-hundred-pound transvestite dance on a tabletop at La Coupole in Paris. I've seen drugged hippies by the hundreds nodding off in Istanbul. I've watched would-be movie starlets at the Cannes Film Festival linger for hours over *pastis* on the terrace of the Carlton Hotel hoping some producer would happen along and pay their bill. I once saw a worried convention of artificial cattle inseminators sit tensely in Tangier sipping mint tea as if they suspected it was arsenic. But nowhere—not once! not ever!—did I see anyone in a café writing anything more serious than a postcard.

Not until I arrived in Rome, that is. For it was here that I met Stephen Geller, who, according to my exhaustive, if unscientific research, is the Last Expatriate American Writer who works in a café. (Actually, to be precise, Geller works in two cafés. But that's getting ahead of the story.)

When I first spotted him at an outdoor table in the Piazza della Rotonda, I circled Geller warily, thinking he might be a plant, a piece of local color preserved and encouraged by the Belle Arti commission. I couldn't believe I had stumbled upon the real thing.

I had other reasons to remain wary and to reserve my judgment. For while it was undeniable that the man was writing, he didn't entirely fit my notions of what a novelist in a café should look like. He was well dressed and stylish in the casual fashion of the city. He appeared to be prosperous and cheerful—not at all like a starving artist—and he had a dog, an attentive white Maltese, perched on the chair beside him. But the oddest detail was that he wasn't working longhand, wasn't scrawling passages in a lined notebook. He was, of all things, typing! flailing his fingers at a Brother EP44 battery-powered portable typewriter.

Once I got to know Stephen Geller and his writing, I no longer had any doubt he was the real thing. While still a graduate student at Yale, he had kicked his career off to a fast start when he published a first novel, *She Let Him*

Continue, which was subsequently made into the critically esteemed movie *Pretty Poison.* Three more novels came in quick succession, as did a couple of dozen screenplays, including an award-winning adaptation of Kurt Vonnegut's *Slaughterhouse Five.* He also wrote reviews for the *New York Times* and *Saturday Review of Literature,* did a hilarious column for the *National Lampoon* called "The Disaster Agent," and produced a sound practical book on screenwriting. In 1971, he arrived in Rome to do the script for *The Valachi Papers* for producer Dino De Laurentiis, and here he has remained ever since.

I assumed that it was with his move to Italy that Geller turned into a café writer. But he corrected this misapprehension and told me that long before he became the Last Expatriate American Café Writer, he was the First Domestic American Café Writer.

In fact, the urge to perform in noisy public places those acts of creative imagination that most authors have a difficult time negotiating in silence and solitude came at an early age to Geller. The son of Harry Geller, a trumpeter, composer, and arranger for Benny Goodman and Artie Shaw, he grew up in southern California, and since his bedroom was right beside his father's studio, he soon got used to doing his homework to the accompaniment of the big band sound, ringing telephones, and nonstop commotion. In college at Dartmouth, he discovered he couldn't study in the library or a quiet dormitory and took to preparing for classes in a restaurant. When he went to the Yale Drama School for his M.A., he began writing at a café on Chapel Street in New Haven.

By the time he reached Rome, his work habits were deeply ingrained, and he ensconced himself at the Café de Paris on Via Veneto, one of the settings of *La Dolce Vita,* Fellini's cinematic dissection of the city's bizarre high life during the fifties. But by the seventies, the place had the low-life look of a B movie, and hookers of various sexes were constantly interrupting Geller, asking him to serve as an interpreter between them and potential customers.

"I found myself in a very dubious position," he says, understating the problem.

Uncomfortable in the role of pimp, he moved on to the Café Greco on Via Condotti, following in the footsteps of Keats and Shelley, Dickens and Thackeray, Hawthorne and Twain, Ibsen and Goethe.

At the Café Greco, waiters have, since 1760, taken a proprietary interest in artists and writers, referring to each as *nostro professore*. They were attentive, even protective of Geller, and would save his table and prevent people from disturbing him. "It takes approximately a week to break in a café," Geller says. "But once broken in, it's family."

Eventually, he switched family allegiances and transferred his "office" to the Piazza della Rotonda, the colorful, car-free square in front of the Pantheon where an Egyptian obelisk with cryptic markings soars majestically above a splashing Baroque fountain. Now like some ancient pagan, Geller orchestrates his schedule according to the rising and setting sun, following its warmth and light from Bar di Rienzo, where he works in the morning, to Bar Rotondo on the other side of the piazza, where he works in the afternoon. Meanwhile, all around him teems the life of the square that the Gault Millau guide, indulging in only slight hyperbole, describes as "worthy of Fellini. Half-naked beauties, pickpockets, street hawkers, introverts, extroverts, freaks and oddities of every ilk heap abuse on each other in an irresistible, spontaneous commedia dell'arte."

Geller concedes that even in this histrionic crowd, the sight of a man banging out books on a Brother EP44 with a Maltese sitting nearby does attract attention, especially from kids who gather around. At such times he feels "quite silly, like a character out of a De Sica movie, with these street urchins looking at this machine." But he says, "Nobody disturbs me unless I want them to."

A CLEAN WELL-LIGHTED PLACE . . . SORT OF

Geller likes company and believes that working in a café is a way of warding off the loneliness and depression some authors feel when confronted by blank pages. "Occasionally you surface," he says, "and look around and see what's happening on the street and then dive back down into the depths of your characters. I would suggest that those writers who find it difficult to write take themselves immediately to a café and work there. I think they'll discover if they find it difficult, it's because they're not concentrating. If you go to a café, you have to concentrate. You can find out a hell of a lot about yourself sitting at a café."

Asked whether it wouldn't be cheaper to rent a room to write in—after all, a day's worth of cappuccino and sandwiches at a café can't be cheap—Geller admits that he gets "a professorial rate." Both bars, proud to have a writer on the premises, give him a discount, and he estimates his monthly bill is no more than $75. "Where can you rent an office for that?" he asks and goes on to explain that the piazza "is a full-service facility." In addition to bringing him what he wants to eat and drink, the waiters cash his checks, take phone messages, look after his dog, and pass along handicapping tips on the races at the local track.

While seeing himself in the tradition of classical café writers and, at the same time, breaking new ground with his state-of-the-art equipment—he's now in the market for a Brother TC 600—he doesn't take himself so seriously that he can't play the straight man for a running gag. He tells of the time Gore Vidal—who lives near the Pantheon—was passing through the piazza and spotted Geller and his dog and said, "Now I know. Now I know who does your writing. You're just taking dictation. You're ghosting *The Tale of Fluffy.*" Every time he went by after that Vidal paused to ask the dog, "What chapter are we on now, Fluff?"

Finally, Geller's feeling for the piazza, this loud, milling place with its many layers of history and mystery, is unlike that of any other writer for the room or office where he works. Quite simply, the spot is for him touched with magic.

No writer, Stephen Geller observes, can reasonably ask for more. But having found his Clean Well-Lighted Place, he doesn't claim sole ownership. There's plenty of room in the piazza, he points out, plenty of cafés in Rome, and so many stories remaining to be told.

* * * * *

CAMPARI AND COMPLEXITY
AT CENTER COURT

The seasons in Rome sometimes advance so slowly, so subtly, that their changes can't be felt any more than can the rotation of the earth. Only the effect, not the process, is perceptible. On a morning in late May one is apt to wake and abruptly realize that another spring is about to pass into summer, and one gets an overwhelming urge to hurry outdoors and seize the day.

Some head for the beaches at Ostia, others settle for a stroll in the Borghese Gardens. Setting out on my own annual rite of spring, I snake my way up the Tiber, swept along by a tidal wave of traffic that thunders beneath a colonnade of plane trees. Leaving the historical center of the city, I cross the river and arrive at the Foro Italico, site of the Italian Open tennis tournament.

A fair club player myself and a frequent commentator on the foibles of that curious subculture, the international tennis circuit, I attend the Italian Open every year, partly to watch the matches, primarily to witness—and participate in —the far more fascinating spectacle that swirls around the periphery of the courts. If a city as multilayered and complex as Rome can be said to have a microcosm, then the Italian Open is it, for the tournament compresses into a single week the essential elements of a 2,700-year-old metropolis that calls itself eternal, yet displays the frenetic energy of a fruit fly living only for a moment. All the Roman hallmarks are here—dazzling color and motion, dense golden light, copious food and wine, high fashion and low comedy, spontaneous friendship and rabid nationalism, grace under fire and ham-handed evocations of a real and imagined past.

Approaching the Foro Italico, one receives conflicting impressions of order and anarchy. The order is entirely architectural and not very interesting except as an example of high Fascist style. Constructed in 1935 during Benito Mussolini's regime, the buildings and statues and a tall obelisk, which still bears Il Duce's name, were intended to remind the public of the grandeur of ancient Rome, which the dictator hoped to re-create. Now the broad slabs of marble serve as cool benches or as billboards for graffiti.

The anarchy is infantile and unconscious, and while it doesn't appear to perturb Italians, it can be daunting to anybody who sets a high premium on linear reasoning. In the parking lot drivers follow patterns and jockey for places in a manner few Americans can imagine. At ticket booths and entry gates, where members of other nationalities naturally start a queue, Italians stand in a jostling, amorphous cluster.

Once past the gates, the crowd spreads out and there's ample room to observe the sport and the fashion show. It would be difficult to say who is more elegantly dressed, the players or the spectators—many of them wear the same outfits. Designer tennis clothes, in bold stripes or clinging pastels, are synonymous with Italy, and no place are Fila, Ellesse, Tacchini, and Cerruti products better displayed than at the Foro Italico, where style, the creation of a *bella figura*, seems as important to fans as winning is to the players.

Bordered by Viale delle Olimpiadi and Viale dei Gladiatori, the red clay courts are set in amphitheaters sunk below street level, and the torrid air that fills these hollows is thick with pollen, perfume, and the aroma of garlic and oregano from a nearby restaurant. Above the Campo Centrale, the main show court, loom massive white marble statues of athletes. Interestingly, they are all—even the skier and the ice skater—naked. With the construction of temporary stands at the top of the stadium, these statues give the appearance of comically inverted Peeping Toms who, while nude themselves, gaze through the steel underpinnings of the bleachers into an area of completely clothed people.

On my first trip to this court, an immense man with an even more immense voice stood up between games and sang parts of arias. Friends swore to me it was Pavarotti urging on Adriano Panatta, who was then the national champion.

Not all of Pavarotti's countrymen are as artistic in encouraging their local heroes, and the history of the Italian Open has been pockmarked with bizarre incidents.

On a number of occasions, players have retreated from the Campo Centrale rather than suffer the outrages that the crowd and the Italian officials sometimes feel compelled to commit in support of their idols. In 1976, Harold Solomon defaulted in the semifinals after getting a string of flagrantly unfair calls. Two years later, José Higueras, a Spaniard with a reputation for impeccable manners, walked off when spectators began hurling insults and coins. A day later, when Adriano Panatta played Bjorn Borg, the Swede held an unassailable advantage. He was used to having people throw money at him. Promoters and advertisers had been doing it for years. When Italian fans slung coins at Borg, he coolly pocketed the cash and beat Panatta.

The field courts lie at the bottom of an enormous oblong cavity styled on the lines of the Circo Massimo, Rome's ancient chariot racecourse. Screened off from each other by cypress hedges, these courts are lined by tiers of gently terraced bleachers surfaced with marble that has sprouted wildflowers and tufts of moss. Serious sunbathers stretch out here for hours, keeping one eye on the tennis and the other eye out for strolling vendors who sell mineral water and ice cream cones.

True aficionados tend to remain standing on the walkway that circles the courts. This way they can move from match to match, catching a crucial point here, a sensational shot there. This also allows them to stay under the Umbrian pines that canopy the footpath. Up there in the shade the air is mild and fragrant, the essence of spring. But down on the courts, summer arrives early, and during long, hard-fought rallies players shed rivulets of perspiration that speckle the red clay with what looks like blood. One can't help being reminded of bullfights. Guillermo Villas, the Argentinian ace, has described the Italian Open in terms worthy of any matador facing death in the afternoon: "The sun is hot. The court is slow. The balls are heavy. It is not easy."

Fortunately for fans, they are free to retreat from the competition, sit under a striped umbrella, and sip Campari. Or else duck into one of several restaurants and watch a different act of commedia dell'arte. Say what you will about Romans and their indifference to northern notions of efficiency—they certainly can choreograph a meal. If the food sometimes falls short of excellence, the show is never less than world class. As in France, eating here is a kind of religious ritual, but it's low church rather than high, closer to a fundamentalist revival than to a solemn benediction. Each course is heralded by loud hymns of praise or blame, the clatter of dropped cutlery and plates, the fast-forward ballet of white-jacketed waiters shouting *"Momento!"* or *"Subito!"* while they hurry off, never to be seen again.

With the arrival of coffee and cognac, the restaurant grows relatively quiet. There's just the background murmur of agents and tournament officials talking deals, the muted sound in the distance of tennis balls thwocking against tight gut, and the clopping of hooves as mounted police patrol the parking lot.

Somnolent and soothing though it is, this clip-clopping of horses alerts anyone who is of a mind to notice such things that the area is aswarm with carabinieri and armed troops in flak jackets. By one of those screwy coincidences that abound in Rome, tennis at the Foro Italico can claim no better than second billing. Nearby, on Viale delle Olimpiadi, in a gymnasium barricaded by sandbags and armored personnel carriers, the Italian murder trial of the century has been taking place for the last three years. Dozens of Red Brigades terrorists are testifying about the kidnapping and assassination in 1978 of Aldo Moro, the former prime minister. It's as though John Hinckley, President Reagan's would-be assassin, were arraigned in a locker room at Flushing Meadow during the U.S. Open.

At the Italian Open nobody appears to find this upsetting. Rome, after all, touches Janiculum, the hill named for Janus, the two-faced god whose gaze falls in opposite directions. Anyone who lives here must learn to look both ways, treating comedy and tragedy as inseparable aspects of every experience.

• • • • •

SUMMERTIME, AND THE
LIVING'S AL FRESCO

Rome is an outdoor city and Romans are inclined to be exuberant public performers. At no time is this tendency truer than during the summer, when, as Eleanor Clark remarks in her marvelous book, *Rome and a Villa,* the streets here constitute "a great rich withinness. . . . Even a tourist can tell in a Roman street that he is in something and not outside something, as he would be in most cities." For foreigners the result is often an immediate attachment to the place and its people. While a stroller in London or Paris has a sense of witnessing a contemporary pageant in a historical setting, visitors to Rome soon find themselves feeling like participants in a daily melodrama.

Many streets are as narrow as hallways, as steep as staircases, as dim and cool as cellars. Yet even where these cramped passages open into broad avenues and roomlike piazzas full of people, Romans maintain their inalienable right to do outdoors anything they might do at home. They don't just eat and drink al fresco. Roosting for hours in open-air cafés and trattorias, or in chairs they have dragged onto the street from their living rooms, they read, watch TV, nod off for naps, put on makeup, brush their hair, pluck chickens, shell peas, sew and knit, play cards, carry on intense, histrionic conversations, engage in even more intense and histrionic foreplay, and sometimes perform still more basic bodily functions. Romans simply like to do things together; they enjoy sharing with the world the endless wonder they take in themselves and in one another.

As thousands of women have found to their displeasure or delight, there is among some Italian men a temptation to carry this sense of togetherness, this urge to share themselves, a little too far. On buses and street corners, in crowds everywhere, they rub up against women and let their hands rove. But in my opinion, there is something impersonal, almost involuntary, about this touching. It shows how after years of living at close quarters men can become terribly confused. Uncertain of the precise contours of their own bodies, no longer capable of understanding where they end and someone else starts, they feel compelled to submit all flesh to a crude braille.

Another troubling aspect of the affinity Romans feel for street life is the affection they have for the cars with which they share their streets. It is not just that they love driving everywhere at a harrowing high speed, so that homey, back-alley neighborhoods and august Renaissance squares all reverberate with the earsplitting harmonics of a Formula One race. It is not simply that they seem to take sensual pleasure in polishing, fondling, and tinkering with automobiles. It is not just that whole families will park in the middle of the city and sit for hours chatting companionably, eating lunch, or reading the Sunday papers. It is not simply that even out-of-town picnics are likely to take place at the edge of a highway, where everybody eats with one eye on the countryside and the other on the cars roaring past, as if bucolic joy can never be separated from the dubious pleasures of the road.

No, it goes far beyond any of this. Like those Spaniards

who look forward to annual fiestas when they release bulls in their streets and then run with them—not *away* from them, but *with* them—Romans appear to delight in living, as Hemingway would put it, "close to the horns." Ignoring crosswalks, oblivious to red and green lights, quick, supple youths as well as dignified senior citizens go dervishing through the thunderous traffic, risking mortal danger, letting sharp fenders pass an inch from their flanks. With all the grace, courage, and inventive footwork of matadors, they hold the hard-charging cars at bay with waves of the hand that would mesmerize any bull.

At Largo di Torre Argentina, a major crossroads for buses and a blaring chaos of converging traffic of all types, the air is so fouled by exhaust fumes it stings the eyes and grates the throat. Yet the crowds keep coming, staring off toward the eye of the storm, where there stand the ruins of four temples, a tall brick tower and its handsome loggia, several truncated pillars and fluted columns, and a copse of cypress and pine trees that have somehow survived the pollution, sinking their roots deep into stone.

When the sun is out, brightening the colors, warming the cats curled sleeping on marble slabs, this spot strikes me as a reassuring symbol of the city's long history, and the local people and tourists who congregate at the square are like solemn witnesses of what has endured and will always endure in Rome. But on overcast days, when the air closes over it like a heavy lid, Largo di Torre Argentina seems a fitting scene for a stoic to contemplate. Cars, buses, and motorcycles career around the classical remains with all the brutal indifference of scavengers scuttling past meatless bones. *Tempus fugit,* and the tourists, dressed in the flashy plumage of birds of paradise, appear poised to fly with it.

If my response to Rome sounds capricious, it is because the city itself is infamously fickle and illusory, and in summer its atmosphere can change as swiftly as the weather. Several years ago, during the dead hours of a July afternoon, I was slumped under an umbrella at an outdoor bar in Piazza di Santa Maria in Trastevere. Aside from a sleepy waiter and me, the place was abandoned, the town paralyzed by heat and dull light. Normally this square displays all the subtle variations of the city's earth tones—ocher, saffron, mustard, terra-cotta, and burnt sienna. Now it was washed out. On the church façade opposite us, even the gold-leaf mosaic of the Virgin Mary and attendant figures had been blanched by the sun. In the center of the piazza, the fountain was broken, its basin dry. The cobblestones glinted and shimmered like ingots of melted iron. There was no noise, no movement. Rome seemed at rare peace, all its people indoors, eating, sleeping, or making desultory love.

Then suddenly a shrieking siren ripped a seam through the closely woven fabric of the afternoon. I came bolt upright, wondering what was wrong, expecting the police or an ambulance to arrive. The waiter didn't look worried. Still, he moved next to my table while the siren wailed on and on, rising, then falling, then rising again. Finally a fellow in an undershirt stumbled out of a building, sauntered across the square to a Mercedes, and fiddling with something under the hood, killed the noise.

The waiter smiled wearily. "A burglar alarm," he said. "The national anthem of Italy." For me his wisecrack was enough to lift the weight of the long, leaden day.

On summer evenings, after a siesta, most of Rome is looking for just such a lift, as well as a breath of cool air. Crowds of pedestrians climb the city's hills to watch the sun fall and dusk gather in milky hues of orange, purple, and ultramarine. Some prefer the Pincio, others the Aventino. I hike up the Janiculum Hill to the esplanade in front of the Fontana dell'Acqua Paola. Below it Rome stretches toward the horizon, a landscape of cupolas, arches, and red brick ruins glowing in the rosy light.

I don't mean to imply, however, that I have this lovely spot to myself. Tourists arrive by the busload and snap photographs of the fountain, which with its water-spouting gargoyles and towering Corinthian columns is heralded by the guidebooks as "the Baroque at its most serene and loving." Italians, on an easier and more familiar footing with their cultural heritage, park near the basin, dip sponges into the swirling water, and wash their cars. Or else they soap down their pet dogs, then send them splashing into the pool for a bath.

Darkness rouses Rome rather than easing it toward sleep, and night noises come on, steadily rising in volume, like electric appliances controlled by a timer. Few pay the ceaseless roar any attention. It affects most Romans as little more than acoustic cologne, the Muzak of the Mediterranean, another signal that the streets are thronged again. Couples stroll arm in arm; young bloods cruise by in their cars, radios booming; kids whir past on skateboards or motor scooters. Flower vendors, musicians, and beggars work the cafés and restaurants.

In this season, my favorite time of day comes very late, often not until hours after midnight, when the traffic on side streets and piazzas has subsided. At last it is quiet enough to hear the fountains, hear the Tiber purling between its marble-faced banks, hear the city's pulse. I move to the middle of the street and lean back my head. As I set off walking again, I stare straight up, seeing through unshuttered windows beautiful beamed ceilings, gilded scrollwork, candlelit vaults, murals of angels and saints and the resurrected Christ, and arching just out of reach, the star-strewn summer sky. Although I may at that moment be returning to my apartment, I cannot help recalling Eleanor Clark's comment that "in Rome to go out is to go home."

• • • • •

THE STAYING POWER AND
THE GLORY

Nights are no longer so tender in Antibes. Although the
village hasn't taken on the tawdriness of Miami Beach or the
tackiness of southern Spain, it has, like every resort along
the Côte d'Azur, changed drastically in the decades since
Scott and Zelda were here amusing themselves and horrify-
ing the French by smashing crystal, wrecking cars, and
falling down stairs. Perhaps it is simply that these days the
rich aren't so different from you and me. In summer it seems
half of Europe has descended on the Riviera, and tourists
rattle into town on motorbikes and Renaults rather than in
Rolls-Royces, and they stay in condominiums and threadbare *pensions* instead of at the Hôtel du Cap or private villas.
Their rubber rafts and runabouts bob brazenly in the paths
of mighty yachts, and their bodies, bared to the legal limit
and basted with Bain de Soleil, have the impudence to turn
as bronze as any jet setter's.

That evening as I left the Grande Corniche and headed
for the coast, traffic advanced through the walls of Antibes
like an army of ants. The maze of streets in the Old City was

clotted with cars, choked with exhaust fumes, and as I circled past the port searching for a parking place, I noticed hot dog stands, snack bars, and everybody, regardless of age or shape, dressed in blue denim.

On a quieter street occupied almost entirely by a modern apartment building, I found the address and pressed a buzzer. The door opened electronically, and from a bare, antiseptic lobby, the kind that gives a look of impermanence and impersonality to air terminals, I went up to meet the man who is often called the greatest living novelist in the English language.

Graham Greene is tall, well over six feet, and looks much younger than seventy-three. If he does stoop slightly at the shoulders, it is not as if bowed by years but as though to incline his ear and listen closer. Only his eyes betray his age. Moist, large, and often fixed on something in the distance, they also seem sad. But then they have seen a lot. I apologized for being late, and blamed the traffic I had run into returning from an exhibition of Nicholas de Staël's painting in St. Paul de Vence.

"There's where he killed himself, you know." Greene waved through his living room, out the double doors, to a narrow balcony. But he was gesturing toward the town ramparts. "He jumped off the wall. It doesn't look high enough, but it worked."

He led me onto the terrace to have a look. Though we stood four or five floors above the street, the noise was nearly deafening, and we had to raise our voices.

"The traffic goes on until all hours," Greene lamented, "and everyone in the building has a barbecue on his balcony. They keep me up half the night chattering over their dinners. Some mornings I'm almost too tired to work."

What time did he start working? How long did he stay at it? I asked, sounding like the rawest amateur hoping to discover some secret in the details of his schedule.

"I'm usually awake by six and keep going until I have a hundred words. That means about five hours. I have to be strict with myself or I'd never get anything done. I used to write five hundred words a day, but as I got older, I found that was too much. So I cut down to three hundred, then to one hundred, just to keep my hand in." When he smiled, his eyelids creased and the moistness of his pupils seemed about to spill out. "I never lose track of where I am. Sometimes I stop smack in the middle of a paragraph."

Difficult as this was to believe, Greene swore it was true. "Of course I used to work much faster. Back when I was young, I liked to bring out a new book every year. It was a conscious reaction against the Bloomsbury people, most of whom seemed content to do a few things, build a huge reputation, and rest on it. But even then I always had to revise my novels again and again to get them right. Now it takes me years to finish a book, and sometimes it still isn't right."

I remarked how strange it was that practice and experience didn't make life much easier for a novelist. "You'd think once a writer had been through it a few times and developed confidence in his talent . . ."

"One has no talent," Greene interrupted. "I have no talent. It's just a question of working, of being willing to put in the time."

♦　♦　♦　♦　♦

As we stared off silently at the wall where de Staël had killed himself, I thought about how Greene's modesty, his insistence on privacy, and his refusal to accept more than the most grudging credit for his accomplishments set him apart from so many writers of this century. He is roughly a contemporary of the flamboyant American authors Fitzgerald and Hemingway, who are always associated with the south of France and with Gerald Murphy's enclave at Antibes. (The same generation produced Faulkner, Wolfe, and Steinbeck.) In those days Hemingway had taken as his motto the French aphorism *"D'abord, il faut durer."* To accomplish anything, one first had to last. And yet it is Greene, a discreet, self-effacing Englishman, who has lasted and continued to write—five hours, every day, one hundred words —while others burned themselves out, died young, committed suicide, slipped into obscurity, or let themselves ossify into literary landmarks.

In 1973, when his most recent novel, *The Honorary Consul,* was published, it received worldwide acclaim and quickly became a best-seller. But apart from the commercial and critical success, it was far more remarkable that a sixty-nine-year-old novelist was still performing at the height of his powers, still writing from first-hand experience about the Third World and revolution, still pursuing ultimate questions about life, death, and belief. In a sense, *The Honorary Consul* can be seen as a companion piece to *The Power and the Glory,* a gauge of the political and philosophical distance the world has traveled in the last four decades. Whereas the priest in *The Power and the Glory* overcomes his cowardice and preserves his faith despite the religious persecution of a left-wing military dictatorship, the priest in *The Honorary Consul* becomes a revolutionary and abandons the Church which has allied itself with a right-wing military dictatorship.

The turnabout surprised some readers. "It shouldn't have," said Greene, whose sympathy has always been with individuals, not dogma. "The book doesn't contradict what I wrote earlier. It only expresses my feelings better. It's rather a relief not to have to be told that my best work lies thirty or forty years in the past. Every time I pick up a newspaper and read about another political kidnapping, I think *The Honorary Consul* may have been a few years ahead of the times."

Greene has long had this sense of timeliness, an instinct for stories that afterward seem prophetic, and a tropism for troubled corners of the world. In Africa, in Saigon and Hanoi, in Malaysia, in Haiti, in Central and South America, he has produced not only dozens of novels, short stories, and travel books, but controversial articles on the Mau Mau uprising in Kenya, influential reviews of hundreds of movies and books, and interviews with Ho Chi Minh, Diem, and Castro, a record which even Oriana Fallaci would envy.

Age hasn't stopped Greene, nor have success and celebrity compromised his integrity. He won't hustle his books and he refuses to withdraw to the comfortable embrace of any of the universities which have offered him sinecures.

◆ ◆ ◆ ◆ ◆

From Greene's novels most readers know something of his experiences in revolutionary Mexico in the 1930s, wartime West Africa in the 1940s, more wars and insurrections in East Africa, Malaysia, Cuba, and Indochina in the 1950s. But throughout the 1960s and on into the 1970s—Greene's sixties and seventies as well as this century's—he has continued to travel, to grow with the times rather than rail at them, and to put himself on the spot.

In 1967 he was in the Sinai, pinned down by artillery fire across the Suez Canal. In August 1968, he hurried to Prague to support Dubcek and protest the Russian invasion. While other writers grumbled and wondered about general conditions in South America and the specific situation in Allende's Chile, Greene made it a point to go there every year, monitored as usual by the CIA. ("We're waiting for you," an American voice warned him by telephone his first night in Santiago.) Then in autumn of 1973, when *The Honorary Consul* was about to appear in America, he refused to do a promotional tour and instead flew to South Africa, where it had been arranged for him to hold secret meetings with various rebel groups.

It would be difficult to think of any author who has written more often and more effectively about the bankruptcy of colonial and post-colonial regimes, the abuses of political power, the threat of unrestrained intelligence agencies, and the repression of personal and religious beliefs, whether by the left or the right. In a world that likes to pay lip service to writers who are fiercely independent, politically *engagé*, and who risk great danger to do their jobs, no one except Solzhenitsyn—certainly not Hemingway, Camus, Malraux, or Sartre—can make the kinds of claims which, interestingly enough, Graham Greene declines to make for himself.

As the lights in Antibes began to blink on, we went inside. The living room walls were lined with books, but there was very little to suggest who lived there. Perhaps the personal memorabilia are in Greene's apartment in Paris or his house on Capri. Or then again, maybe he prefers to keep his personal life tucked away, his day-to-day existence unencumbered by the past.

While Greene mixed us each a Scotch and Perrier ("You Americans like ice, don't you?" This American did), I told him I had always enjoyed his books, but admired even more his energy, courage, and commitment. He dismissed the compliment, saying straight out that he was a coward. He was frequently afraid and suffered from a long list of phobias. "I'm terrified of water, for example. Always have been. It's all I can do to splash my face in the morning and rinse away the shaving cream."

As he proceeded to tell of spending months in Tahiti, scuba diving every day in a vain attempt to conquer his fear, I pointed out what appeared obvious. It was a triumph of bravery to spend hours in the ocean if you were pathologically afraid of water. Greene shook his head. He was still a coward, he said, even though he'd forced himself to go diving. In a way it was a replay of his attitude toward his talent. Inverting the biblical homily, Greene in effect claimed you couldn't judge him by his works but only by the weaknesses he felt within. Perhaps this paradigm of his reasoning explained the paradoxical nature of his fictional characters, who have to be strong because they know they are weak, who are good because they are sinners.

♦ ♦ ♦ ♦ ♦

After the discussion of cowardice, there came an uncomfortable moment and we quietly sipped our drinks. Greene has a reputation of resisting interviews, being uncooperative in conversation and chary of personal disclosures. It may simply be that people hold unrealistic expectations of writers and assume that anyone whose medium is language must be perfectly at ease in conversation. But the connection between the spoken and written word is tenuous at best, and many novelists, loquacious though they may be by nature, have learned the hard way to avoid idle conversation with journalists.

"It's gotten so I hate to say who I am or what I believe," Greene admitted. "A few years ago I told an interviewer I'm a Gnostic. The next day's newspaper announced that I had become an agnostic."

For Greene, anecdote appears to provide a more comfortable vehicle for exploring past experience and a most effective means of communicating with strangers. Certainly he is seldom as animated or interesting as when he is telling a story. When, to break the silence, I said I liked the painting on the wall behind his couch, he explained it had been a gift from Fidel Castro and suddenly we were launched for several hours.

Greene had visited Cuba while Castro and his men were fighting in the mountains, and through intermediaries, he managed to contact the rebels and arrange a meeting. When the interview went well, he asked if there wasn't some way he could return the favor, and Castro had said yes. Come back and talk again and bring warm clothing. It was cold in the mountains, especially at night, and his men were freezing.

Since Greene suspected he was being watched by Batista's police, he didn't see how he could smuggle supplies over the circuitous route to their rendezvous point. There was also the danger of compromising his journalist's neutrality.

But Castro convinced him he didn't need a truckload of contraband, just sweaters, pairs of socks, and trousers. Greene could wear several layers of clothing and take them off after he arrived. Nobody would notice, and even if they did, Greene could claim he was cold. Weren't the English always cold, even in the tropics?

So Greene bundled up like an Eskimo, suffered through the sweltering heat of the lowlands, reached the mountains and molted a few layers of clothing, then returned to Havana pounds lighter.

Years afterward, when Castro was in power, Greene came back to Cuba, presumably more appropriately dressed for the occasion. It was then that Castro presented him the painting in gratitude for his help during the revolution.

I asked if Cuba had changed much, and he said, "Oh yes, for the average Cuban it's a far better place. But . . . well, it's too bad about Havana. It used to be such a lively city. Now it seems sort of dreary."

Then abruptly we were discussing Haiti. Perhaps there was a transition. If so, I was unaware of it. Yet I had no sense that Greene was taking tangents. For one thing, as an accomplished raconteur, he had the ability to control a listener just as skillfully as he sets up a reader. His hands, in particular, he used to good effect, clasping them in his lap, then letting them fly out at dramatic moments. For another thing, there was a kind of cartographical logic to his vignettes and he connected distantly spaced dots on the map and circled the globe as unerringly as a latitudinal line.

I myself had once been in Port-au-Prince during what was

described as an abortive coup. Electricity was cut throughout the city, tourists were hustled into their hotels, and ill-tempered troops patrolled the streets. Only later was it revealed that Papa Doc Duvalier, trapped in the bathroom during the course of a family squabble, had pressed an emergency button to signal his guards to rescue him from the john. As a comic Caribbean dictator, Duvalier might have been invented by Greene's friend Evelyn Waugh— if, that is, Papa Doc hadn't been deadly as well as ridiculous.

"Did you know, I put him in the publishing business?" asked Greene. "After *The Comedians* came out, Duvalier went into a rage and threatened to get revenge. But rather than order one of his voodoo priests to put a hex on me, he had somebody write up a crazy attack on me. A whole book of nonsense privately printed at Papa Doc's expense. I'm really rather proud of it. I went to a lot of trouble to get a copy and I wouldn't part with it for anything." He found the book and passed it to me. A collage of photographs, forged documents, and lunacy, it sought to portray Haiti as a tranquil and progressive paradise, and Graham Greene as inaccurate, dishonest, and an infamous racist.

"I wish Papa Doc had come over to the British West Indies. I would have introduced him to what may be a branch of my family, descendants of my ancestors who owned plantations there. They're black. One little boy has my name."

We moved, not unnaturally it seemed, to a discussion of movies. He still likes films but no longer sees as many as he did when he was a critic for the *Spectator,* and he doesn't much care to be around movie people. It's been years since he's taken the short drive up the coast to Cannes for the film festival. And yet, not long ago, he made a surreptitious screen debut.

Near Antibes, François Truffaut shot *Day for Night,* a movie whose subject was essentially the difficulties of making a movie. As the original title suggested—*La nuit améri-*

caine is the technique for filming night scenes during the day—Truffaut meant to show how cinematic verisimilitude depends on mechanical devices, how actors, for all their foibles, can produce art, and how illusion can lead to truth.

When one of the actors in the movie within the movie is killed, an insurance agent flies down from London to determine whether a claim should be paid and the film should proceed or be canned. The insurance agent has a bit part, but a pivotal one, and Truffaut, dissatisfied with all the professional actors available, put out a public call for an Englishman of a certain age. Graham Greene saw the advertisement and auditioned for the role under an assumed name. Truffaut was favorably impressed; this Englishman seemed authentic, just the sort to play a seedy calculating insurance agent.

Only later, as Truffaut was watching the rushes, did someone in the screening room moan, "My God, that's Graham Greene." At first Truffaut was angry and upset that during his lighthearted exploration of the relationship between illusion and reality he had been duped, a victim of his own illusions; then he was embarrassed that he hadn't recognized Greene, a writer whose work he admired. Truffaut telephoned, apologized profusely, and promised to cut the scene. But Greene said there was no need for apologies, he had enjoyed himself and wanted to be in the movie. In that case, Truffaut assured him, he could count on seeing his name in the credits.

No, Greene didn't want that either and made Truffaut swear he wouldn't mention his name. "I was curious to see if anyone would notice," Greene explained. "Very few did, and I was delighted by the secret."

Although *Day for Night* was released in the United States virtually at the same time *The Honorary Consul* was published, he never exploited the incident. Content to enjoy his secret, he called no press conferences, provided no self-serving leaks to news agencies. One can only surmise how another novelist might have acted under the same circumstances.

♦ ♦ ♦ ♦ ♦

It was inevitable, I suppose, that I would eventually try to work the conversation around to Vietnam. Greene knew the country and conflict as few people did, having gone there before Dien Bien Phu and defined the tragedy taking shape for America long before the Marines arrived, before Tet and the truce and the spring of 1975's sudden unraveling. But at this subject, his volubility faltered. He could do an imitation of Diem's hysterically high-pitched laugh, and he told a final, self-deprecating tale, this one about his meeting with Ho Chi Minh, which had made him so nervous beforehand that he smoked a pipe of opium.

But as for the war itself, and America's military policy, he had little to say. What was there to say that he hadn't said before? In the opinion of most experts, *The Quiet American* is still the best novel about the war, and when one considers that it was published more than twenty years ago, it seems all the more appallingly prophetic. So Greene would only repeat that he loved the Vietnamese and especially the city of Saigon, which in those days had a laundered look each morning and smelled flowery and full of life. When asked if he'd like to go back, he said he preferred to remember it as it had been.

The scent of charcoal smoke had insinuated itself into the room. Out on the balconies everybody was barbecuing. It promised to be a long, restless night and a difficult morning for Greene. As I got up to leave, I asked what he was working on now. I had waited until the end so he would feel free to duck the question. But he said he had recently picked up a novel which he had set aside years ago. Although he was making progress, he wasn't sure he would finish it or how it would turn out if he did. "I put the book away when that Kim Philby business blew up. I was well into it by then, but there are certain similarities between my plot and the Philby affair, and I didn't want anyone to think I had drawn on that. There has already been enough nonsense about my friendship with Philby. Perhaps now the novel can be read on its own terms."

◆ ◆ ◆ ◆ ◆

As we headed for the door, he added that he was also collecting some of his autobiographical sketches. A sequel to *A Sort of Life*? I asked. Not exactly. Not exactly. Just isolated pieces and a few articles that still seemed worthwhile to him.

In the hall now, I said if the anecdotes he had told me were in the collection, it was bound to be a fascinating book.

"I don't know. Interesting experiences, fascinating people you meet in extraordinary places—of course that's all very enjoyable. But they don't make one a better writer and they don't always make for good books." As we descended in the elevator, Greene went on, "I sometimes think failure and boredom, the feeling of loneliness, of being flat and empty, have more influence on a novelist."

When we reached the lobby we shook hands, and then I was out on the street, wondering about the final paradox Greene had presented. In the elevator he seemed to have been suggesting that although he wrote successful and compelling novels, it was out of a sense of failure and boredom; although he had led an exciting life, it was just an effort to overcome a feeling of hollowness and drift.

But it seemed to me Greene had indulged in self-deprecation one time too often. If anything had become clear that evening, it was that Graham Greene is a good man because he has always had a moral compass, a courageous man because he is willing to go where the compass points, and a gifted writer because he has the ability to make the reader understand and follow the compass too.

The town of Antibes may have changed since Fitzgerald, and all those who came after him, prowled this coast searching for some vision of grace and dignity that would endure after innocence ends. But Graham Greene has lasted and will last.

♦ ♦ ♦ ♦ ♦

SYMBOLS OF ROME

Rome has its predictable symbols—St. Peter's, the Forum, the Colosseum, and the Spanish Steps. But to anybody who has lived here awhile, these are no more than stock footage from a travelogue, trite material for postcards, banal backdrops for photos. A native scarcely notices them. If pressed to offer the perfect emblem of his city, a Roman would more likely name a variety of scenes and sights that go unnoticed by visitors.

As many have observed over the centuries, the essence of Italy is illusion raised to the level of an art form. Very little here is what it appears to be. Or, to be precise, nothing is as it appears to be at first glance. Elaborate trompe l'oeil represents a basic architectural principle in Rome, and the most arresting examples are better symbols of the city than those changeless chunks of marble left over from the classical era. The Church of Sant'Ignazio, for instance, seen from inside, seems to have a huge dome decorated with frescoes of the *Entry of St. Ignatius into Paradise.* Look more closely, however, and you discover that the ceiling is flat. Andrea

Pozzo, the Renaissance artist who painted the frescoes, conjured up a convincing impression of a dome on a flush surface.

Francesco Borromini created an even more dramatic optical illusion in the Palazzo Spada. From a courtyard, one gazes down what seems to be a very long corridor to yet another courtyard where there stands an enormous statue. In fact, the corridor is only thirty feet in length and the statue is the size of a pygmy. Borromini has played a clever trick with perspective.

The lessons of artists and architects long dead have not been lost on contemporary property owners who refuse to let petty considerations such as reality or the law prevent them from completing their own masterpieces. The Via Appia Antica, the ancient road once trod by Roman legions marching south, is a historical zone that the Belle Arti commission has declared strictly off limits to new construction. But ruins that have been discovered on private property can be reconstructed and inhabited. As a result, many a rich Roman has bought a parcel of prime real estate on the Appia, secretly buried old bricks, potsherds, and marble slabs, then bribed some corrupt archaeologist to "excavate" the stones and swear that at the height of the empire an important villa stood on the spot. Having satisfied the authorities, the owner then has built to his specifications the pink stucco extravagance he has had in mind from the start. With a swimming pool and tennis court, the place is likely to resemble a house in Miami Beach or Beverly Hills and bear no comparison to the grandeur that was Rome.

Call it a symbol, call it a survival instinct, but it is certainly striking that Romans invariably look both ways on a one-way street. And in piazzas that are supposed to be closed to cars, knowledgeable residents exercise special vigilance, well aware that such squares are generally swarming with every motorized vehicle known to mankind. Those inclined to absentminded strolling are apt to be blind-sided by a truck, more likely than not traveling at high speed in reverse.

Reverse gear might itself serve as a fitting symbol of the city. Surely, it is never used so often or so inventively in any other urban area. When Romans miss a turn or an autostrada exit, they think nothing of backing up for blocks, even miles, to rectify the error. One night at 2 A.M., I was taking a baby-sitter home when a man in a Lancia started racing me up Viale Trastevere. My hands were clamped to the wheel and I was sweating bullets. He was smoking, chatting with his wife, glancing in the rearview mirror, whizzing along in reverse at forty miles per hour.

But maybe Rome's horrendous traffic is so well known, so much a part of the local scene, it is now just another hackneyed instance of tourist folklore. To find a truly meaningful symbol one must readjust his sights and focus on out-of-the-way corners and odd bits of arcana. With that in mind, I have compiled the following list, the fruit of a decade-long search for the city's ultimate emblem.

In the portico of the Church of Santa Maria on Cosmedin there hangs the *Bocca della Verità*, the famous bas-relief of a face with a frightening open mouth. In the Middle Ages, according to Georgina Masson, this was "used for a sort of trial by ordeal to see if people—particularly wives suspected of unfaithfulness—were telling the truth." The legend held that if anyone told a lie while his fist was thrust into the gaping mouth, the jaws would slam shut, snapping off his fingers. But considering the jaunty disregard with which most Romans treat sexual fidelity and truth-telling, it shouldn't be surprising that the Mouth of Truth has no teeth. At worst, it would leave a gum print and a little saliva on a liar's hand.

At the Foro Italico, where the Italian Open tennis tournament takes place every May, center court is surrounded by monumental marble statues of nude athletes. No fig leaves here. Even the skier beside the scoreboard is naked. To my mind, there can be no more graphic example of an elementary Roman attitude—if you've got it, flaunt it.

It must be remembered, though, that while this city is a worldly center of hedonism, it is also the home of the Vatican, the Holy City, and it is full of nuns and priests. The secular population, concerned with style, takes its fashion cues from Via Condotti. But the clerics, too, have their sartorial shopping districts. On Via dei Cestari the store windows display a wide range of ecclesiastical clothing, and smiling mannequins model nuns' habits, priests' vestments, cassocks, surplices, and even modest, sensible canonical underwear.

One of the charms of Rome is that many outdoor cafés and trattorias are surrounded by shrubs and flowers—potted palms, delicate begonias, geraniums, great clusters of blooming oleander bushes. But a closer look frequently reveals that the plants are chained together, then chained to the pavement, to window ledges, or to iron grillwork. Thus two of the city's characteristic obsessions are combined— the deep, unquenchable thirst for beauty and the equally deep appetite for security. The thieves here, perhaps driven by their own impulse to possess fragile beauty, will not only swipe plants from cafés, they will take flowers off tombstones. Some of these are then wrapped in cellophane and sold by Gypsy children who work the most popular tourist spots.

On a trip to St. Peter's, my eleven-year-old son stopped in a souvenir shop and brought back a lethal-looking switchblade knife. To put it mildly, I was unamused and I was in the process of insisting that he throw it away when he pressed the button and a plastic comb, not a glinting blade, flicked out of the handle. With a few strokes, he raked his unruly hair into place. Suddenly, I thought, here it is in a young boy's hand—the consummate symbol of the city, a switchblade knife that turns into a comb. It seemed to me every Roman male's fantasy come true, a clever melding of make-believe menace with serious narcissism.

But in this city, there is always something new to learn, some hilarious humiliation to experience, some other reminder to a foreigner that essential facts that might define the place usually remain a mystery until it is too late. On a recent evening my wife and I went out for dinner and ordered thick slabs of *bistecca alla fiorentina.* When my wife couldn't finish hers, I asked the waiter for a doggy bag. He resisted the idea, at first acting confused, then incredulous that I meant to carry off part of the meal. But I carefully, yet firmly, repeated that we were going to take the leftover steak home to our dog.

In point of fact, we don't have a dog. In point of fact, I intended to eat the meat the next day for lunch. But there was no need for the waiter to know this. All he had to do was follow my instructions and wrap up the last bloody slice of *bistecca.* Finally, he shrugged and cleared away our plates, returning from the kitchen with a neat package covered with aluminum foil.

Next day at noon, I took the steak from the refrigerator and unwrapped it—to find a yellow congealed wad of fat and bone. There wasn't a shred of meat. Naturally not. The waiter was no fool. If I insisted on carting restaurant food home to a dog, he'd follow my instructions literally and pack up a few scraps for Fido. But the *bistecca alla fiorentina* he had no doubt turned over to the chef, who'd ground it up for today's pasta.

• • • • •

THE MAYOR OF ROME

Late last winter in New York City, at a reception following the widely hyped appearance of Norman Mailer and Gore Vidal at a benefit for the writers' organization PEN, Gay Talese introduced Mayor Ed Koch to a short, sturdy man wearing designer glasses with tinted lenses. "I'd like you to meet Mickey Knox, the Mayor of Rome," Talese said, and the fellow's title caused Koch to do a comic double take.

Mayor Koch had visited Rome and met his counterpart there, who didn't bear any resemblance to this grinning, impish guy Talese was introducing. In addition, Rome's elected mayor certainly didn't speak English with a Brooklyn accent. But as thousands of expatriates and tourists can attest, Talese wasn't joking. For a generation of Americans, Mickey Knox has served as the real, if unpaid, Mayor of Rome. Although he seems to wear the mantle of his office with gruff good humor and casual disregard, he takes his responsibilities seriously. Gregarious and outgoing, he is a master at greeting newcomers, bringing together people from wildly disparate backgrounds, brokering business deals, discovering ways to evade the Eternal City's infernal tangles of red tape, wangling discounts for friends, finding hotel rooms and apartments, and serving cold drinks and very hot chili at his apartment on Via Gregoriana, just up the street from the Spanish Steps.

Since he is not a man of independent means and does not receive the municipal stipend he so richly deserves, Knox finances his public life by working in Italy as an actor, a dialogue coach, scriptwriter, translator, and occasional producer. Had the course of twentieth-century American political history not taken an ugly turn, he would probably have remained in Hollywood, and with a long list of lead parts to his credit he would now be playing character roles. But after having gotten his career off to a fast start by doing fifteen movies in succession, Knox was blacklisted during the McCarthy era in the early fifties. "There was an ad taken out," Knox explains, "opposing the reelection of State Senator Jack Tenney, who was in charge of the Un-American Activities Committee in California. Everybody who signed his name to that ad was automatically blacklisted."

Unable to find film roles, he returned to New York, entered the Actor's Studio under Lee Strasberg, and performed on stage and in summer stock. But even though he could no longer get work in Hollywood as an actor, Knox had other skills that were needed on the West Coast. He spoke French and Italian. When Anna Magnani was cast in *The Rose Tattoo,* Danny Mann, the director, asked Knox to work as Miss Magnani's dialogue coach—a demanding task, since the movie was shot in English, a language that was a complete mystery to Miss Magnani.

Knox was so successful at tutoring Anna Magnani, he soon began to get other assignments, some in the States, many in Europe, where he could act as well as coach dialogue. Eventually he wound up in Paris, playing a part in the film *A View From the Bridge* and coaching the lead actor,

Raf Vallone. "Then I got the longest job," he says, "on a picture called *The Longest Day.*"

♦ ♦ ♦ ♦ ♦

He loved living in Paris and was content to stay on there. But he was married at the time to Joanne Morales, the sister of Norman Mailer's second wife, Adele, and she hated the place—especially the cool, haughty Parisians. "The proverbial straw that broke the camel's back," Knox remembers, "came one day when she was shopping for shoes. She tried on a pair and said they were too tight, and the saleslady said, 'Madam, it's not the shoes. It's your feet.' Joanne burst into tears and said, 'That's it! We're leaving.' So we moved to Rome."

He has lived there ever since, working in a variety of capacities for a series of what he admits were mostly forgettable B pictures. He co-produced a couple of spaghetti Westerns and did the dubbing scripts for many others. Since these films were originally shot without sound and the actors recited nonsense rhymes while histrionically performing their roles, Knox had to invent long stretches of dialogue, including a few crucial passages in that classic of the genre, *The Good, the Bad, and the Ugly.*

Once the blacklist was no longer an issue, Knox accepted an occasional role in the States, where he was, in his words, "a new old face." He appeared in two of Mailer's movies, *Wild 90* and *Beyond the Law,* and has often had guest shots on such television shows as "Hart to Hart," "Quincy," and "Archie Bunker's Place." Most recently, he played in Mailer's *Strawhead,* an off-Broadway production about Marilyn Monroe. Friends, agents, and directors have urged him to move back to America permanently and resurrect his career, but Knox prefers the people and the pace of life in Italy. "In Los Angeles," he says, "everybody eats dinner at five-thirty and goes to bed by nine—just when I'm ready to have a drink and go out to a restaurant."

Then, too, he realizes he has an obligation to his office as arranger, fixer, expediter, social arbiter, and oral historian of Rome. For all its size and surface bustle, it is a fairly quiet and provincial city, and Mickey Knox runs the closest thing to an international salon—although he would, no doubt, prefer to think of it as a saloon. When Burt Lancaster, Ava Gardner, Shelley Winters, Marlon Brando, Kirk Douglas, Eli Wallach, Anne Jackson, Albert Finney, Liv Ullmann, Elizabeth Taylor, Susan Sarandon, or Ben Cross come here to work and play, Knox breaks out the booze, cooks up a pot of chili, and organizes evenings that usually include members of the Italian film community, visiting writers—Joseph Heller, Pete Hamill, Terry Southern, Bruce Jay Friedman—scholars and artists from the American Academy, and wide-eyed and innocent tourists, especially tall young blondes whom he happened to bump into that day at American Express.

No one else in Rome manages so consistently to reach across social and cultural barriers and bring together in his living room the likes of Franco Nero and a ceramics engineer from Pittsburgh; Adele Chatfield-Taylor, a director of the National Endowment for the Arts, and a *Playboy* photographer; film director Martin Ritt and an oil attorney from Houston; Bernardo Bertolucci and a Jesuit priest, who diplomatically doesn't mention *Last Tango in Paris*.

Shortly before becoming American ambassador to West Germany, Richard Burt came to town to get married on the Campidoglio. When Knox learned that the Burts intended to go to a tourist trap on the Via Veneto for their wedding dinner, he stepped in and took charge. Knox orchestrated the entire affair at a local trattoria, arranging for flowers, a special menu, and champagne.

"The champagne was extra," he says, proudly recalling the accomplishment. "But the meal was 15,000 lire [about $10] a head."

Perhaps his most impressive achievement has been remaining on friendly terms with a few of the most fiercely

81

competitive literary figures of the post-war era. He remembers walking up New York's Eighth Avenue in 1953 with James Jones, Norman Mailer, and William Styron, and watching Styron throw his arms around the other two and gleefully announce, "Here we are, the three best young writers in America!"

But as the euphoria of that moment later degenerated into raucous drinking bouts, deadly serious arm wrestling, and even more deadly backbiting, Knox found himself caught between warring camps. Through it all Knox not only refused to take sides, he kept the lines of communication open between combatants, and he derives some satisfaction that Styron, Mailer, and Jones got back in touch.

If all this makes Mickey Knox sound like the saintly product of a union between Perle Mesta and Santa Claus, it should be remarked that while he is usually an affable and generous man, he can also be crusty, rambunctious, ribald, and combative. In short, he doesn't restrict himself to throwing parties. He throws other things—and his aim isn't always perfect.

Once at a reception at Gore Vidal's villa in Ravello, perched on a cliff high above the Amalfi Coast, Knox stunned a crowd that included Luigi Barzini, Italo Calvino, a couple of movie moguls from MGM, and a six-foot-three-inch black transsexual. He did this by expressing his disdain for a jacket worn by Freckie Vreeland, son of former *Vogue* editor Diana Vreeland. When Freckie took off the jacket, Knox tossed it out a window, whence it sailed like a hang glider toward the beach a thousand feet below.

On another boisterous night, this time at a restaurant surrounded by friends, Knox got into a dispute with William Murray, who was in Rome to do one of his Letters for the *New Yorker*. While Murray took issue with him over some now long-forgotten point, Knox was tossing a salad—in a bowl about the size of a bushel basket—for the entire table. As he added liberal splashes of oil and vinegar, Murray repeated, "Mickey, you're wrong. You've been abroad too long."

Finally, Knox replied, "I ain't never been a broad," and with that he picked up the barrel-sized salad bowl and slung its greasy contents in Murray's general direction. Celery and carrots sailed everywhere; olive oil drenched people two tables away; tomato seeds freckled everybody's face; mozzarella hit the wall and left snail tracks as it slid to the floor. A great silence settled over the room. Mustering enormous dignity under the circumstances, Murray brushed the roughage from his lapels, left a fistful of lire to pay his part of the bill, and stalked out of the restaurant. Then Donald Stewart, a European consultant for *Playboy*, broke the quiet with a line that many feel should be inscribed on Knox's tombstone. "Waiter," Stewart called out. "I want to speak to the manager. There's a salad in my fly."

Now, years later, having made up with William Murray and paid off dozens of laundry bills, Knox laughs about the incident. He doesn't exactly admit he was wrong, he doesn't precisely apologize. But when asked by various writers and editors why he doesn't do a book about his life, preserving this and the dozens of other anecdotes that crop up in his conversations, he shakes his head and says, "I can't. I just can't. I don't wanna hurt people. I couldn't write the truth about them till they were dead." He chuckles. "I mean I wouldn't even want to do it till I was dead."

Then, too, of course, Mickey Knox has to consider his constituents. There's little time or inclination to look back when he's so busy doling out patronage, arranging introductions, and orchestrating events in his city.

♦ ♦ ♦ ♦ ♦

CAT CITY

Whenever I return to the United States and happen to mention that I live in Rome, people are more apt to talk about the cats than they are to inquire about Italian politics, classical studies, Catholic theology, or even the food and wine. Many visitors seem to remember this city as little more than a mildly interesting stage set against which a truly fascinating feline drama is played out day and night. If they recall the Colosseum or Trajan's Forum or Largo di Torre Argentina, it is only as a showcase for cats more variegated than any fevered artist's mind could imagine.

In her eloquent book *Rome and a Villa,* Eleanor Clark devotes almost a dozen pages to cats and describes their ancestral homes in the ruins as "a botanical garden of exotic furs, in every combination; marmalades shading to bronze, orange in trout specklings on grey or black, a single contrasting or striped forearm on a monotone coat, every kind of bib and dashing including the common chest triangle, often only one perky ear of solid color like an insistent strain of nobility through the conglomerate birth."

Speculating on how so many of the city's historical sites came to be inhabited by hundreds and thousands of cats, Clark muses, ". . . it may be only that cats are a mysterious animal as everyone admits, and Romans are alert to mysteries outside their nature and fall easily into ways of propitiating them. Or perhaps they came into honor as a check to rats carrying plague in the Middle Ages. . . . No doubt there is some element of primitive religious sense, or call it superstition, at the root of the matter." Cats, she adds, "are a link with the past, that is, with all time, having kept a clearer set of original instincts together with more various personality than any other tamed animal."

Clark goes on to remark upon the irony that while cats here are left to live where they choose and are often fed by slightly goofy old ladies called *gattare,* who cook up plates of pasta and put them out like votive offerings for gods, most Italians take cats for granted and wouldn't dream of petting, stroking, fondling, or talking to them as foreigners do. Although Roman felines appear to occupy "a unique position among the public cats of the world," Eleanor Clark notes that "there are not many private ones—a Siamese in the house is apt to be a sign of neurosis or international marriage; normal Roman life has no more need or use for pets than for similar attachments within its own species."

This point was driven home to me with particular emphasis a few years back, when American novelist Mark Helprin moved here to live while he was putting the final touches and a high glossy polish on his best-seller *Winter's Tale.* Helprin and his wife Lisa took in an alley cat that had been badly mauled in a fight. Its wounds wouldn't heal, and they brought it to a veterinarian, who refused to believe they were willing to pay him to treat such a mangy creature. He suggested they set it loose and let it live or die among its own low-bred kind. When the Helprins insisted they meant to keep the cat and take it back to New York City with them, the vet became more incredulous. "Why, this is as if an Italian moved to America and adopted a wounded cockroach as a pet. Cats are like insects. They should be left outside to clean up the garbage."

To the world's cat lovers this may sound hideously hard-hearted, but to a Roman it makes pragmatic sense. It's not that local citizens don't care about cats. It's just that the most intense currents of their emotions run along different lines. While they might consider it a waste of time and money to nurse a sick stray and while they don't have a tendency to go misty-eyed with sentiment at the sight of a kitten, they can become quite exercised when the question of cats is linked to larger issues and more powerful passions, such as politics and conspiratorial theories.

Recently there have been vague rumblings about a severe decline in the city's cat population. Although no one has taken an accurate census—in fact, estimates of Rome's human population are dubious—rumor has it that the cats are dying off. Or else they are being transported out of the city or even killed off by civic authorities.

Those inclined to believe the worst about their elected officials feel that a secret political deal has resulted in an equally secret and scandalous cat roundup. According to this scenario, the cats have become so fat and happy, they have lost all appetite for rats and are more than willing to live cheek-by-flabby-jowl with the rodents they were supposed to exterminate. As the cats and rats reproduced geometrically, the threat of disease increased along with their offspring. Some areas of the city, especially in the historical center, started to reek like immense boxes of Kitty Litter. While tourists enjoyed the sight of entire piazzas carpeted in living, moving, meowing cat fur, the people who had to live there weren't amused. Thus, in the dead of night, the government sent out squads of men hell-bent on trapping and transporting cats to the suburbs.

Cooler heads and scientific types offered the opinion that this move to the suburbs was a natural phenomenon, not at all a government policy imposed on an unwilling cat populace. In a migratory pattern that sociologists and demographic experts could plot on a graph, cats, it was said, had chosen to follow humans out of the congested and polluted *centro storico,* away from the cacophonous noise and choking smog, to the peaceful suburbs. There they lived in tranquil communities, safe from traffic and the traumas of the fast-lane, high-stress life. True, these new neighborhoods were lacking in traditional charm and personality. But that was precisely their point, their reason for being. The people and cats who had chosen to live there were sick of Italy's excess of personality, fed up with Rome's charming eccentricities, and were more than willing to trade their sprightly life in the ruins for a bland paradise of quiet, cleanliness, and privacy.

But while this explanation satisfied those Christian Democrats who favored free enterprise and believed that the laws of the marketplace could account for everything, including population shifts, there were others who made an equally cogent case that the cats would never have dispersed to the suburbs if the municipal authorities had dealt quickly and forcefully with the problems of crowding, pollution, and traffic control. Communists charged that high rents and low wages had driven the working class out of the city, and the cats, always fellow travelers, ever eager to show solidarity, had gone with them. What's more, inflationary food prices and miserly pensions had killed off the *gattare.* Fewer and fewer crazy old crones were willing to prepare mounds of pasta for the cats when they couldn't afford to feed themselves. No resolution of the decrease in the cat population was possible, the Communists claimed, without sweeping changes in the ownership of the means of production and a drastic redistribution of the wealth. (Interestingly, no populist demagogue suggested, à la Huey Long, that the people should kill off the fat cats and spread the grease.)

Naturally, in a Catholic country and in a city that surrounds the Vatican, the issue of declining population touches a raw and tender nerve. Some people fear that a birth-control policy has been imposed unilaterally on the cats. Although this might sound a trifle paranoid, it has to be kept in mind that there is a precedent for this sort of biological depredation being visited upon an Italian animal population. Two years ago in Venice, the city fathers decided that there were too many pigeons in Piazza San Marco, and they took prompt prophylactic measures. They laced cornmeal with anti-fertility drugs, then scattered it around the city for the unsuspecting pigeons. If it happened to birds, people wondered, what was to prevent it from being done to cats?

There was no definitive answer to this question or to dozens of others regarding the presumed cat decline. Indeed, for all that was written and said about the problem, there was no objective evidence to prove that it existed. Instead of hard data, each interest group and party on the broad spectrum of Italian politics continued to assert opinions as if they were unassailable truths. What seemed to matter most was theory, not practice, short-term partisan advantage, not long-run solutions. Just as no one offered any documentation to show that the cats were declining in numbers, nobody took steps to protect or rescue those that remained.

In fact, in the final analysis, the debate appeared to have a lot more to do with Roman politics and personal obsessions than it did with cats. As Italians talked about the felines, they were probably doing what people the world over tend to do—trying to work the conversation around so that they could talk about themselves.

But in this deafening echo chamber of human babble, who speaks for the cats?

Well, perhaps Steven Brint does. With tongue in cheek and a Cheshire-cat grin on his lips, he has recently drafted a learned paper on the subject. A member of the Sociology Department at Yale University, currently a scholar in residence at the American Academy in Rome, Dr. Brint has pondered the matter for months and come to some sound, if puckish, conclusions that will reassure those who feel the

Eternal City should always include a substantial number of felines.

Yes, it is true [Dr. Brint writes], the cat population of Rome *has* declined, but not at the rate suggested by some observers. There are two reasons for this: the adaptability of cat society and new forms of cat provisioning in human society. We see a lot of self-help in the cat community: cats staying up extra hours—moonlighting, if you will—to supplement the food they have managed to obtain during the day; a measurable increase in the degree of stealth and material cupidity among the feline; and, paradoxically, also a greater willingness to double up on rations and a decrease in the size of territories that are defended against interlopers. We also see a slow process of suburbanization as cats move out from the *centro* seeking new food supplies. The Largo di Torre Argentina and the Forum may be relatively depopulated, but the cat population in Monteverde and other outlying areas is booming.

On the human side, the demise of the *gattare* seems to have brought out a latent (and one would have thought extinct) love of cats in the rest of the Roman population. People have taken up the slack by picking up strays and feeding them for a few weeks or months before letting them shift for themselves again. I like to think that we have moved from a system of oligarchical control in cat provisioning to a sort of foster care system.

The effects of these changes are still unknown. I see a new surliness and rootlessness in the cat population—which is what you would expect from a foster care system—but that is just an impression. In any event, we do know that the demise of the *gattare* has not meant the demise of the *gatti*. The city is still teeming with them, though they may be a little redder in tooth and claw than before.

• • • • •

MOVING? DON'T EXPECT A NEW LEASE ON LIFE

All around the world, discussions of real estate tend to share something in common with war stories, fishing tales, and anecdotes about sexual exploits. Invariably they start with an assurance that sets off warning bells of doubt bound to deafen all but the most gullible listener. "This is the truth. It actually happened."

Forgive me if I repeat the same tired bromide, but I have no choice. Believe me, honest to God, this is gospel truth, *la vera verità*, as Italians put it. Renting an apartment in Rome is like no other agony that afflicts modern man.

I should know. I have lived in twenty apartments scattered across the city and have moved a half dozen times in the past seven years. I have leased a luxurious flat in Via Boncompagni, have huddled in an odoriferous hovel above a horse stable, suffered the shrill harmonies of traffic in the *centro storico* and enjoyed the tranquil terraces of villas overlooking the Doria Pamphili gardens. The common denominator of these and all my other Roman residences was that I rented them on a short-term basis.

90

Now I am moving again. No, I'm not a nomad, not a felon fleeing the law or a bankrupt running out on the rent. I'm a married man with over a hundred boxes of books, and I have two sons who own approximately thirty-seven thousand dollars' worth of plastic figures from *Star Wars* and the *Masters of the Universe.* It is doubtful that Napoleon's invasion of Russia involved more luggage, demanded more logistical planning, or resulted in more emotional damage than my family's annual forced march.

Why do we do it? The reason is simple. It is just very difficult to explain to anyone who hasn't lived in Rome.

The city has a rent-control law called Equo Canone. A fiendishly complicated, even if originally well-intentioned piece of legislation, it was meant to impose strict guidelines on the lease price of every property so that people, especially in the densely populated and popular *centro storico,* would not be abused by speculators or avaricious landlords. In theory, this law did not just set down financial terms. It established a uniform code for rental agreements and it spelled out the limits of a landlord's right to raise prices and to evict tenants.

As might have been predicted by advocates of an open market, the inevitable occurred. Property owners became increasingly reluctant to rent apartments at artificially depressed prices to people who then might refuse to move out for years, even decades, after their leases expired. And just as predictably, standing tenants fought every attempt to dislodge them, for they feared that they would never be able to find another place to live. Urban experts now estimate that over one hundred thousand Roman apartments have been left empty and off the market because their owners don't care to abide by Equo Canone. At the same time, nearly three hundred thousand eviction notices have been served and are trickling through a court system that can take five years to settle a civil dispute.

An entire legal industry has cropped up around Equo Canone. There are lawyers who specialize in protecting landlords and in prying people out of apartments. There are other attorneys who represent tenants and who spend much of their working day measuring floor space, counting steps, doing architectural and historical research, then advising people exactly how much they are being overcharged.

According to an abstruse formula that would tax the mathematical ingenuity of Einstein and the patience of the Dalai Lama, a new apartment costs more than an old one—except when the old one is located in a building classified as "historical." In that case the landlord can charge a much higher price—unless the building has no elevator, no central-heating system, no view, and no terrace, in which event the rent must be reduced by increments that have to be calculated by the kind of computer that spits out the throw weight of rockets and the gravitational pull of distant galaxies.

It is left to overworked magistrates to make Solomonic decisions as to whether a janitor can be construed as a doorman, whether a fireplace qualifies as central heat, and whether a slot-like window opening onto a dim airshaft can pass as a scenic view of an ancient courtyard. The same magistrates have to judge whether tenants whose leases have long since lapsed can be booted out if there is an invalid, a nursing infant, or a dying senior citizen in the apartment. One often gets the impression in Rome that the old, the ill, and the odd newborn infant are shifted from family to family at the first sign of an eviction notice.

Now it might well be asked how foreigners and, more specifically, Americans fit into this infernal system. The answer is, they don't. That is to say, Americans almost never find apartments that are offered under rent-control conditions. Instead, they wind up with the sort of contract that has repeatedly sent me and my family reeling from one new address to another. After holing up in hotels and searching for months, they are forced to rent apartments on the black market and to accept larcenous markups, under conditions reminiscent of those that provoked the serfs to rebel in Russia.

My most recent real estate calamity was by no means atypical. We had rented the top two floors of a palazzo. Downstairs, there were two bedrooms, two full baths, a fireplace, a large living room furnished with antiques, and a kitchen equipped with a close approximation of modern conveniences. Upstairs, there were two terraces and a quiet studio where I worked.

But the place wasn't without drawbacks. The rent ran four times the legal rate, and the building had no elevator. We had to climb ninety-seven steps to the lower floor, then twenty more to the terraces.

The high rent and the daily Himalaya treks I could take with only minor anxiety and respiratory attacks. It was the other conditions that created problems. The landlady insisted we move out for two months during the summer—she knew that if we remained in the apartment a full twelve months, we would qualify for rent control—and we had to allow her daughter, a college student, to live in the upstairs studio for two weeks at Christmas and two weeks at Easter.

Still, we were satisfied, especially since we knew many people who paid a lot more for less room, and under far more troubling circumstances. Some friends had had to put down a year's rent in advance. Some had leased gutted shells which they had had to renovate at their own expense. Others were paying a steep price for the privilege of baby-sitting apartments stuffed with the owner's books, papers, clothes, and personal effects. Almost everybody was flying blind, operating without the protection of a legally enforceable contract, depositing the rent in hard currency in the owner's Swiss account or dispatching it to a postal box on some exotic offshore island.

For instance, Pat Conroy, author of *The Great Santini* and this season's best-seller, *The Prince of Tides*, recently returned to Rome after two years in the United States. More than willing to sink a goodly portion of his royalties into the right apartment for his family, he rented a splendid place overlooking Piazza Farnese. Or, to be precise, the splendor is in the flat's potential.

It is large and bright and blessed by a breath-catching view. But when Conroy moved in with his wife and four children, he discovered that the Italian diplomat who owned the apartment had not only failed to repaint it, as promised. He had furnished it with four mattresses on the floor and two lonely armchairs in the living room. Although there were three telephones, not one of them worked, and the toilet was cracked.

"I can live with a certain amount of this aggravation," Conroy says. "I've rented apartments here before and I know what to expect. I don't mind paying an extortionate price and we'll eventually get the place furnished. But when we went to sign the lease, I found out the owner refused to list the actual price. He said that that has to be a secret agreement between us. Yet I had to give him a notarized assurance that I'd vacate the place at three months' notice. In exchange he gave me a verbal promise that we'll be able to stay for three years. I feel like a guy that just bought an underwater lot in Port Alligator, Florida."

By comparison, we counted ourselves lucky and thought we had finally found a home. But then we returned after our annual two months of forced absence and discovered that our duplex apartment had become a monoplex. Having blocked off the top floor, the landlady tearfully explained that her daughter had been stricken by tuberculosis and needed to recuperate in my studio, on our two terraces. When we suggested that a sanitarium might be a more appropriate spot for the poor girl, her mother began wailing. When we timidly hinted that it was only fair that after losing half our apartment we should receive a fifty-per-cent reduction in rent, she went into hysterics. Imagine an aging diva singing *Aida* and tearing at her hair, and you have the basic picture. When she choked back her sobs, mopped off her mascara, and grudgingly gave us a ten-per-cent reduction, we capitulated.

Two weeks later, the landlady's daughter experienced a miraculous recovery and returned to college. We, however, were not allowed to return to the top floor. Instead, a French-woman moved in and entertained a succession of gentlemen callers. When I complained to the landlady, she claimed that I had voluntarily agreed to vacate the upstairs in exchange for a reduction in rent. I calmly replied by cutting off the heat and electricity to the studio. She just as calmly met this challenge by jamming matchsticks into the door locks on my car.

Then I made my worst mistake. I hired a lawyer and threatened court action. There followed a harrowing few months of psychological warfare and gutter fighting that ended with the landlady and her attorneys on one side of a broad gleaming table and me and my lawyers on the other side, signing documents of the same thickness as the Manhattan telephone directory. Don't ask me how it happened. I don't know. But whimpering and nerve-damaged, I yielded more ground than Roosevelt at the Yalta Conference.

I suppose there is a more or less happy ending to this story. I learned a lot about Italian law and I increased my Italian vocabulary, especially my grasp of certain flavorful idioms heard mostly among Neapolitan dockworkers. Education, as Saul Bellow has said, is everybody's second prize.

Eventually, I also located a new apartment. It's really not such a bad place, even if it does overlook a discount tire dealer. Of course we're paying far more than the market value, we have no written contract, we were forced to put down an immense damage deposit, and we have to fork over the rent in untraceable cash for which it would be pointless to demand a receipt. But only one thing bothers me. The landlord insisted that a room, which he refers to as "our dead father's office," be kept locked and unused. Although

I have never seen it, he tells me the room contains the deceased man's desk and books and papers.

I suspect otherwise. I suspect the "dead father" will someday be resurrected and will reclaim his office. Or, worse yet, perhaps he is already in there, and has been ever since our arrival. One morning he will unlock the door from the inside and send me and my family scurrying and thumbing through the real estate pages for ads that read, "Furnished apartment, for foreigners only. Embassy or corporate references required. Hard currency and sense of humor a must."

◆ ◆ ◆ ◆ ◆

JAMES JONES, AN ELEGY

When James Jones died in May 1977, almost every newspaper and magazine in the country carried a fulsome obitu-
ary or eulogy written by a friend, a passing acquaintance,
even an enemy. Given the general bitchiness of the literary
community, this would have been heart-warming if it hadn't
been bizarre and infuriating. For twenty-five years few serious writers in America got such bad press as Jones—not
simply sniping acrimonious reviews but cheap-shot put-
downs in articles, interviews, and reviews of other writers.
Some of it was perhaps jealousy of the critical and commercial success of *From Here to Eternity.* Much of the rest
seemed to have been resentment of what was supposed to
have been Jones's crudity, his indifference to most elements
of style, personal as well as literary. *Esquire,* for instance,
once named him one of the worst-dressed men in America
because, interestingly enough, he wore Levi's, Indian moc-
casins, and jewelry.

In the last nine years, I spent a total of two or three weeks
with Jones. During that time, we exchanged maybe a dozen

letters and a few more phone calls, so I can't claim to have known him well. And yet in the obituaries, eulogies, and reminiscences there is a crucial omission which no one else appears to have noticed. To quote *New York* magazine (June 6, 1977), "After sixteen years in Paris, James Jones returned to America in 1975 with his wife, Gloria; his daughter, Kaylie; and his son, Jamie. They sold their splendid rambling Paris apartment on Ile St. Louis and bought a big old farmhouse on Sagg Main Street in Sagaponack, Long Island."

♦ ♦ ♦ ♦ ♦

In fact, Jones returned to America in 1974, not 1975, and it wasn't to move in with the literati on Long Island but rather to take a job teaching creative writing at Florida International University in Miami. One can understand why people would want to eliminate that year from Jones's life. It jars; it doesn't fit his image; it doesn't seem to make sense. Why would a writer whose trademark had always been toughness and independence, a writer supposedly contemptuous of critics and impatient with intellectuals, a writer reputed to have been rich—why would such a man teach? And why at Florida International University? Barely three years old and built on the heat-warped runway of the old Tamiami Airport, it's a school for commuters, workies, blacks, and Hispanics. Surely a novelist with so many friends and connections could have found a sinecure anywhere, couldn't he?

All of these questions occurred to me when in the winter of 1973 Jones wrote an express letter and asked me to find him a job. There was no opening at the University of Texas where I taught, but I had a friend, Harry Antrim, chairman of English at Florida International University, and he was interested, if a little bewildered, by the idea of having Jones on the faculty. Not surprisingly, he temporized.

Jones, however, held nothing back. He urged me to press

on and arrange a position for him. Since he hadn't been to college, he had no idea what to expect or what he could demand, and so he insisted that I negotiate every facet of his contract, from salary to teaching schedule.

Meanwhile, Florida International University, having never hired anyone like Jones, had no idea what to expect or to offer. Very discreetly, Harry Antrim posed some of the same questions that had passed through my mind and he asked me to put them to Jones.

With characteristic bluntness Jones told me he was returning to America because he needed money. He had made a lot, but had also spent a lot. The "splendid rambling Paris apartment" was, he explained, his only capital asset; he was trying to sell it, but couldn't find a buyer. Now he was over fifty, in ill health, and anxious to provide security for his family. Living in America, he thought, would allow him to supplement his writing income by teaching, lecturing, giving readings, doing the writer's-conference circuit. Did I have any suggestions? He was available anytime. Whom should he contact? What should he charge? Could I arrange a tour for him in Texas?

Just thirty at the time and with two virtually unknown novels to my name, I was forced to admit I wasn't in the best position to help him, and this led me to inquire obliquely why he had turned to me in the first place. Weren't there other people—friends, acquaintances, agents, literary connections—who could have gotten him a better job at a better school and set him up with a schedule of personal appearances?

The question, of course, was potentially embarrassing, but Jones didn't duck it. Nor did he spare me. He admitted I wasn't the first or only person he had asked for help. He had let a lot of people—good friends of long standing—know what he needed. Most hadn't bothered to reply. Others claimed they couldn't do anything for him. He was on his own, and the clearest proof of this was that I was now his only contact, FIU his lone job prospect. Although he

JAMES JONES, AN ELEGY

sounded a bit puzzled and hurt, he showed no anger or self-pity and said he thought he could do a better job at FIU than at "some fancy New England school."

So perhaps there are good reasons indeed why some people would like to eliminate that year from James Jones's life. It introduces a troubling subtext to the eulogies and orations intoned at his funeral. This seems worth knowing, just as it is worth reporting that Jones apparently did a damn good job of teaching until he sold his house in Paris and at the end of the academic year moved to Long Island.

Although I'm tempted to join the crowd and end by re-creating one of the afternoons I spent with Jones walking the streets of Paris or eating in Vietnamese restaurants or sitting in cafés, I'll limit myself to a single moment that seemed to reveal a side of the man which is too seldom mentioned by those who remember him mostly as a drinking buddy, a teller of war stories, a barroom brawler, or a classic American naïf. One warm fall day we wound up in Les Arènes de Lutèce, an ancient Roman amphitheater, a miniature colosseum on the Left Bank where old men play *boules* where gladiators once fought. A little girl with a pet guinea pig sat near us, trying to get the animal to lie still in her lap. When it came bounding over to Jones, the girl got up, grabbed the guinea pig and gave it a couple of hard whacks on the head. Immediately, Jones was on his feet. *"Mais non,"* he pleaded. *"Ne fais pas ça. Sois gentille."* Don't do that. Be nice.

It is the final phrase that stays in my mind when I think of James Jones—the plea he never would have made for himself, the kindness he extended to everyone, even to those who went out of their way to hurt and insult him. *Sois gentille.* He was.

OFF THE BOOKS, BETWEEN THE LINES

For a week last January, snow fell on Rome's marble ruins and red tile roofs. It snowed again on St. Patrick's Day, once more the next morning, and a final time in mid-April, the week after Easter. As a result of the freakish weather—the worst since World War II—the hills surrounding the city are now banked with dead eucalyptus trees, and in Rome's center, at many of the most popular tourist haunts, the palms are gray-brown. This "big chill," as commentators called it, echoing the title of the popular American film, reminded foreigners that Rome's climate can be quite nasty and its hold on *la dolce vita* fragile.

If the weather weren't enough to make expatriates wonder what had happened to the sweet life, another sort of storm howled through Rome, leaving little visible damage but plenty of lingering doubts. On March 2, Richard M. Heller, a prominent American attorney and tax consultant, was arrested and thrown into a jail bearing the incongruous name of Regina Coeli, "Queen of the Heavens." Charged with a variety of financial malfeasances, he was remanded without bail for preventive detention pending his trial. In Italy people often remain imprisoned for years before a verdict is handed down.

The arrest provoked considerable consternation in the foreign community, particularly among Heller's clientele, which included a large number of the American press corps, as well as many diplomats, artists, and celebrities. Even those who had never met the man felt deep unease at the way the case developed.

The initial investigation had been conducted not by Italian authorities but rather by IRS agents at the American Embassy, who ultimately discovered that they lacked jurisdiction. Under the provisions of a new tax agreement between the two countries, the IRS passed its evidence on to the Guardia di Finanza and urged the Italian fiscal police to take action.

Quite apart from the determination of one man's guilt or innocence, the consequences of this incident could crowd Regina Coeli to the rafters and dramatically change the atmosphere of Rome, a city which historically has been hospitable to expatriates, its agencies lax about holding them to the letter of the law. Many fear that the more efficient and officious IRS will no longer be satisfied with enforcing U.S. tax statutes itself. Instead, it will pressure the Italians to investigate the thousands of Americans who live here off the books, between the lines.

While some of these illegal aliens are students spending a year abroad or tourists who have accidentally overstayed their visas, the majority are permanent residents who have never obtained proper papers or work permits. I am speaking now not of marginal types, but of corporate executives, internationally renowned artists, respected academics, and highly skilled professionals, all of whom have discovered a basic truth about their adopted home: It is often impossible to live here entirely within the rules. For if Rome is seductive, it is also eccentric; if it is fascinating, it can also be frustrating and utterly baffling. Unless you have a heightened sense of the absurd and accept that idiosyncratic conditions and improvised solutions are as much a part of daily life as wine and pasta, you are doomed to chronic worry and probably a hasty departure.

According to law, any foreigner in Italy staying more than seventy-two hours must register with the police and obtain a *permesso di soggiorno,* formal permission to remain in the country. It goes without saying that this law is ignored by millions of tourists. If even a small percentage of them descended on the *questura,* the nation's already sclerotic bureaucracy would suffer a massive coronary occlusion. As it is, Italy's civil servants cannot keep up with the volume of work generated by foreigners attempting to become legal residents. Judging by my own experience, it can take as long as a year to process an application for a residence permit. This means going week after week to a cavernous office, jostling with throngs of understandably upset Third World refugees, and dealing with officials who do not acknowledge that there is anyone who doesn't speak Italian, and the Roman dialect at that.

Even if you survive and win—that is, obtain a *permesso* —you lose. For one thing, you have to undergo the same ordeal repeatedly, sometimes as often as every three months. For another, your name is recorded, denying you your rationale for violating thousands of Italy's unintelligible, anachronistic, or contradictory laws and regulations.

For instance, a registered resident receives a sixteen-digit fiscal code number and must begin filing a tax return on his worldwide income. This may sound reasonable; after all, if one lives in Italy, why shouldn't one pay taxes here? But things *all'italiana* are seldom that simple and straightforward. One does not just declare one's salary, show receipts for income and expenses, then pay a set percentage. Tax evasion is so endemic, so deeply ingrained here, that authorities are given great latitude in "rectifying" returns. In a country where doctors and lawyers routinely declare average annual incomes of about $10,000, scarcely more than they pay their secretaries, and where many shop owners claim to earn less than $5,000 a year, the government starts with the assumption that people are lying and proceeds to levy taxes according to its own recondite estimates. This means that a law-abiding American who acknowledges an income of $40,000 may find himself paying taxes at the $80,000 rate, since few officials believe that anyone would admit more than half his earnings.

Italian tax officials are not alone in operating on the basis of dubious suppositions and unfathomable reasoning. Last year my wife had a minor automobile accident that caused us more culture shock than chassis damage. While our car was at a stop sign, a second car came around a corner in the wrong lane and clipped off a fender. The other driver immediately claimed my wife was at fault and informed us that in Italy, whenever there's an accident involving a stop sign, the driver who is stationary bears all expenses.

Naturally we did not accept this reckless driver's word. I called our insurance agent, expecting him to file a claim and force the offender's insurance company to pay. But no, he explained that his company would have to cover all repair bills since, despite what Italian traffic laws may have to say about guilt or innocence, insurance companies have reached private, informal agreements.

In order to keep cases out of crowded courts and hold down expenses, there's an unwritten rule that in a nonfatal collision, when one driver says he has stopped at a stop sign, it is automatically assumed he was running a stop sign and is therefore responsible for damages—even if someone plows into him from behind.

In a country where personal connections, unwritten agreements, and private arrangements often supplant the law, it is no surprise that many foreigners cope by the simple expedient of never registering with the police, never obtaining a *permesso* or a fiscal code number, never officially admitting that they exist. They are thus relieved of the necessity of getting an Italian driver's license, declaring the value of the cash and personal possessions they import and export, and abiding by dozens of niggling regulations. According to the letter of the law, one is even supposed to register, and pay a tax for, any houseguest who stays longer than three nights.

In another nation, these civil responsibilities may be easy to fulfill, or at least manageable. But in Italy the mechanics of everyday life are so taxing, so time-consuming, something as basic as cashing a check or mailing a letter can devour an entire morning. Forms, it seems, must always be filled out in triplicate, then signed and stamped by an important man who has just gone to lunch. Small change is in perpetually short supply and while customers crowd around counters, clamoring for service, clerks and tellers perform in slow motion some dreamy ballet of aimlessness that would exhaust the patience of a Buddhist monk. I myself have not been in an Italian post office in four years—I would as soon submit to root-canal work. Like thousands of Romans, I send all my mail through the Vatican or have couriers carry it to the States.

Whether because of short-term convenience or absolute necessity, many American corporations and prestigious universities with overseas extensions have long operated in Italy off the books. This in turn has forced their employees to live in the same limbo. Having reached abusive rental agreements, having secretly imported equipment and furniture and just as secretly exported currency, having brought over executives, bureau chiefs, and professors who lack work permits, these institutions don't dare hire anyone who might inadvertently alert authorities that the entire operation is illegal.

Consequently, while these outfits don't have to worry about union wages, pension contributions, medical insurance, fringe benefits, and severance pay, they may occasionally feel they have sacrificed their independence, even their professional integrity.

There are Italians who maintain that the country's confusing laws and endless tangles of red tape act as a kind of prior restraint, a control on citizens and aliens alike and, in extremis, as ready-made justifications for the arrest or deportation of potential troublemakers. Italy may be the only Western country where people are prosecuted not just for crimes but for "exhibiting criminal tendencies."

An economist with highly placed connections in the Socialist party once told me, "Foreigners believe Italy is inefficient. They think the system is flawed. What they don't understand is that the system is designed to be flawed. This keeps a lot of bureaucrats working, and it means that since nobody, not even natives, can live here entirely within the law, everybody is vulnerable, everybody has something to hide."

Whether one regards this as crude cynicism or Machiavellian cunning, the reality is that Rome is full of Americans, famous, infamous, and obscure, who live here illegally and have little choice but to remain so. They pay their bills in cash, sign their names to nothing, and drive cars with American license plates or temporary tourist disks that are years out of date.

One battered Fiat has passed through so many hands in the expatriate community, it has become the common thread that links dozens of disparate lives. It's an old friend one sometimes sees in the street. A 1968 Maine license plate is bolted to the rear bumper; a wooden plaque on the front has been painted to resemble the plate in back.

To anyone who has never lived in Italy, all this may sound dubious at best, downright reckless at worst. When I first arrived in Rome, I confess I was troubled by the constant need for finagling and subterfuge. It seemed not just to cast people into profound legal jeopardy, but to erode some innate sense of self-respect, the sort of pride Americans take in their willingness to announce name, address, rank, and serial number whenever asked. But if one stays here long enough, the Roman aphorism, "Only for death is there no solution," comes to sound comfortable, consoling. *L'arte di arrangiarsi,* "the art of arranging things," becomes a major source of pleasure.

• • • • •
IL SORPASSO

According to conventional wisdom, Italians are a lively and sybaritic people far more interested in enjoying themselves than in working, making money, or becoming entrepreneurs. In the past one seldom heard them described as productive—at least not in the sense of producing industrial goods and services—and most business reports about the country tended to focus on political instability, labor-union problems, and the shaky currency. So it came as a considerable surprise to foreigners—and to some natives, for that matter—when it was announced last winter that Italy had passed Great Britain and now claimed to have the world's fifth-largest Gross National Product.

Late in spring, the nation's economists and statisticians started making a case that the GNP figures didn't tell the entire glowing story. According to their own rather exotic PIL Index (Prodotto Interno Lordo), Italy had also outperformed France and now stood fourth in the international financial sweepstakes. Only the United States, Japan, and Germany were ahead of this land which formerly boasted more about its *dolce vita* than its *vita industriale*. Suddenly film stars and soccer heroes had to accept second billing to business executives, who had assumed the status of sex symbols. In a newspaper poll, Gianni Agnelli, the sixty-six-year-old Fiat chairman, emerged as the man most Italian females wanted to have an affair with.

While word of Italy's great leap forward—local journalists and politicians proudly referred to it as *il sorpasso*—shocked outsiders, the truly startling news was the way the country had overtaken its competitors. In part, it benefited by a decline in oil prices and the drop in the value of the dollar. It also exercised ample measures of energy, ingenuity, and marketing skill. Fiat started producing more and better automobiles, including luxurious Lancias and Alfa Romeos. Luciano Benetton made his family's name synonymous with colorful and stylish sportswear, and Gruppo GFT helped transform the nation into Europe's leading clothing manufacturer. While General Motors and Volkswagen turned to Italian design shops to give their cars more flair, Cagiva, a family-owned enterprise, became the world's top producer of motorcycles outside of Japan.

Still, for all its hard work and innovations, the country might have remained permanently mired in sixth place if it hadn't suddenly seen an advantage in admitting a secret fact of life here—namely, that much of the economy exists underground, far from the prying eyes of business regulators and out of the reach of sticky-fingered tax collectors. As the *Galling Report*, a monthly review of Italian business news explained, "No nation this side of, say, Indonesia, has such a robust 'black' economy." Once Istat, the national statistical office, started to factor in estimates of the business that transpired under the table and off the books, Italy's economic indicators jumped as much as 20 percent.

This underground economy—or *lavoro nero*, as it is called—doesn't simply consist of whole families of unskilled workers producing ballpoint pens and cigarette lighters in basement "factories." Government bureaucrats get off each day at 2 P.M. and many of them then switch to jobs in the private sector, laboring in untaxed anonymity for multinational conglomerates, secret research and development labs, and offshore financial institutions. Foreign firms, including American ones, have been quick to capitalize on this pool of sophisticated workers who are willing to forgo traditional health and retirement benefits in exchange for undeclared and untraceable cash.

Naturally, the English and French have smoldered with resentment at the revised numbers that appeared to put the Italians, of all people, ahead of them. Some complained about voodoo economics, and moralists in the diplomatic community grumbled that it should hardly have been a source of pride for a nation to acknowledge that one fifth of its annual income was generated by illegal activity. It was, they pointed out, as if the United States decided to brag in its agricultural reports about the millions of dollars of revenue generated by marijuana growers.

Italians reacted defensively to criticisms of *il sorpasso* and continued to derive keen satisfaction from their achievement, all the more so because it was based on cunning and creativity. They weren't drones like the Japanese or drudges like the Germans. Any fool could get rich if he had state-of-the-art equipment, robotized factories that resembled space stations, and "new age" executives and plant managers with expertise in everything from double-entry bookkeeping to biorhythms. But it required genius to accomplish the kinds of miracles that are commonplace in Italy. The crumbling and chaotic city of Naples, for example, does not have a single glove factory. At least not officially, not as far as the tax authorities can prove. And yet each year it manufactures and markets more than five million pairs of gloves.

But for every Italian who revels in such success stories, there are two or three wise souls who cautiously remark that all the glorious information about *il sorpasso*—much of it pure speculation—comes from the same government officials whom they have always distrusted and tried to elude.

What if, these doubters ask, it is all a trick, a political conspiracy to justify an eventual 20 percent tax raise to match the estimated increase in the GNP? *Basta*, they say, with this boasting about being richer than France or England. Better to pretend to be poor, better to drink a little wine, eat a bowl of pasta, and even sing "O Sole Mio," cling to the old clichés in public so that in private the engines of commerce can keep humming. These people prefer that the economy remain, to paraphrase Churchill's description of Russia, a secret in a mystery wrapped in an enigma.

What makes this enigma all the more difficult to penetrate is that Italy's formidable First World economy flourishes in spite of a Third World infrastructure. The postal system, for instance, seems to exist not so much to deliver mail as to produce wildly improbable anecdotes with which people regale one another at dinner parties. In addition to stories about letters that arrive months or even years late and about police raids on post offices where 90 percent of the workers were absent, there are truly Kafkaesque tales that might just provide an ironic explanation of the economy.

One such tale is told by Ralph Schmidt and Susan Babcock, a couple of newlyweds who believed they had shrewdly taken the measure of their adopted country and made the appropriate practical decisions. They chose as their pattern Taitu china, which is manufactured in Italy. But since their research indicated it would cost twice as much and take longer to get delivery from Milan than from New York City, they placed their order at Bloomingdale's and had the plates mailed to Rome. "This is so smart and clever of me," Susan remembers thinking.

Sure enough, ten days later, "in good, efficient Bloomingdale's style," Susan and Ralph received a notice that their package had arrived and they should pick it up at the Fiumicino Airport post office. Susan drove there the next morning and spent an hour—by Roman standards a remarkably brief time—searching for precisely the right postal employee who, once found, informed her she was too late.

It was 11 A.M.—closing hour for that section of the post office. Besides, the friendly official explained, she had failed to read the fine print on her notice and had not brought along two notarized and translated copies of her receipt for the goods in the package.

"I thought I had been in Italy long enough," Susan says, "to talk my way through this problem." She showed the man her Bloomingdale's credit card, smiled hopefully, flashing big beautiful blue eyes, and asked whether this sufficed.

The official assured her that it did. Unfortunately the office really was closed and someone else had the only key to the storage room. But now that she had proved to his satisfaction that the package belonged to her, he said he would expedite matters. He promised that the Italian china from New York City would be delivered directly to Susan and Ralph's apartment, a couple of blocks away from Piazza di Spagna. They would have it in two days, three at most.

"I thought, Heaven! I'm in heaven. I've learned to work the system," Susan recalls.

Fourteen days later, when the china had still not arrived, Susan feared the system was working against her again. But at long last another notice did come. Addressed to Ralph, it announced that something was waiting for him at the central post office on Piazza San Silvestro. Convinced that it had to be their china, Susan went to fetch it. But she came up empty again; the postal workers at San Silvestro refused to hand over to Susan what had been addressed to Ralph. After all, they said, what proof did they have that she was his wife and not an interloper who just happened to share the same last name?

The following Saturday morning, they decided the impasse had lasted long enough. Moving systematically on two fronts, Susan drove back to the post office at Fiumicino Airport while Ralph went to the central office on San Silvestro. At the airport, Susan spent several hours ascertaining that her package from Bloomingdale's definitely was *not* there. She personally searched the storage room, and officials persuaded her that the china had been shipped to her home address. If it hadn't arrived there, that meant that it must have been rerouted to the central post office on Piazza San Silvestro.

Since she knew Ralph was at San Silvestro, this greatly relieved Susan. Unbeknownst to her, however, he had gone there and collected a registered letter that informed him that the post office at Fiumicino was holding a package in his name. He was advised to bring with him two notarized translations of his receipt from Bloomingdale's. Naturally concluding that Susan had by now picked up the package, Ralph hurried home to meet his wife, who was anxiously awaiting him and her china. When each saw the other, empty-handed and eager with anticipation . . . well, in short order there were recriminations, raised voices, general aspersions on Italians and specific ones about life in Rome. Then there were tears.

To save the situation, Ralph suggested to his bride that they give up, forget the china and go out for a long and leisurely lunch liberally lubricated with wine. This they did, discovering in the process the best aspect of life here. The waiters, hearing of their predicament, laid on several free bottles of champagne.

At five o'clock that afternoon, they stumbled back to their apartment and found in their mailbox a notice announcing that they had a package waiting for them not at Fiumicino, not at Piazza San Silvestro, but at the post office on Via Monterone, where the initiated know that all sizable parcels arrive. Days later, having recovered from the lunch, they finally got their china. Not a single cup, saucer, or plate was missing. But as they reckoned the damage, it had cost them more in time, money, and dead nerve cells than if they had ordered the Taitu from Milan.

The experience did, however, have a hidden bonus. As Ralph Schmidt sees it, they mastered the secret of the currently high-flying economy. All the business orders and cash payments and credits have safely arrived. The debits and overdue bills are still in the mail. As soon as they reach the right addresses in the coming months, Ralph reasons, Italy's trade surplus will disappear, its balance of payments will level off, its debt load will rise, and its GNP will subside to sixth place. But, meanwhile, he and Susan have gone native and see no point in refusing to join their friends and neighbors in celebrating the delights of *il sorpasso*. After all, as some Roman should have expressed it, life is short, art is long, and economic estimates are a matter of much debate.

PIA ZADORA'S NEVER
AROUND WHEN YOU NEED
HER

At first, I'll confess, flattery played a major role. When RAI-Uno, Italy's oldest and most prestigious national television channel, invited me to participate in a panel discussion on Henry James, I was beguiled by a sense of my own self-importance. Later, I saw a larger cultural significance to the event. Where else but in Italy—certainly not in the United States—would a major network devote half an hour of prime time to a writer who had never run for political office, committed a felony, or signed a multi-picture film deal? And where else would a network pay a guest handsomely to discuss a nineteenth-century author? I congratulated myself for having had the good sense to settle in a noble nation that valued literature so highly.

All too ready to acknowledge that Europeans have a deeper respect for the arts than do Americans, I recalled my most recent promotional tour. For six weeks I traveled the States flogging a book, and my life degenerated into a blur of late-night talk shows followed by early-morning talk shows, strychnine coffee in Styrofoam cups, daunting producers who rushed me in and out of studios, TV hosts with imposing hairdos and pancake makeup, and the annihilating sense that no one anywhere had read a word I or anybody else had ever written. On the final leg of the tour I found myself in Detroit on a show with Pia Zadora and a housewife who had written a tome entitled *How to Teach Your Cat to Smile.* Fearing terminal brain damage, I retreated to Rome.

My debut on RAI, I assumed, would be less hectic and much more intellectually stimulating. Over the telephone, an earnest producer informed me my fellow panelists would be a well-known university professor and an important publisher. My role was to provide an American point of view. The producer also mentioned that Mila Vannucci, an actress, would give a dramatic reading. But I convinced myself this didn't compromise the program's seriousness. After all, James had written plays, and his style, convoluted though it is, depends on the cadences of spoken language.

I arrived at the RAI studios in midmorning, prepared to tape a thirty-minute show to be broadcast, I thought, that evening at six-thirty. The producer, a chain-smoking young lady with disheveled hair and chewed nails, showed me to her office and said we'd wait for the other guests. Again she told me the panel would consist of an actress, a professor, and a publisher. "How shall we identify you?" she asked.

I spelled my name, then pronounced it slowly.

"Not that. I mean what are you? Why are you on the panel?"

"You invited me," I said, baffled.

"We got your name from the American Embassy. They didn't tell us what you do."

"I'm a novelist."

"Published?" she asked.

I told her I had written eight books and that my most recent novel was set in Rome and concerned the Red Brigades, a left-wing urban terrorist group. Her expression changed. I wanted to believe she was impressed. At the very least, interested. Instead she said, "You're not a Communist, are you? RAI-Uno is closely associated with the Christian Democratic party. The theme of our show is Christianity in Henry James."

I assured her I wasn't a Communist. But I feared I had little knowledge of Christian influences on James. True, his plots turned on certain moral choices, but—"Simply discuss those moral choices," she broke in. "We'll speak of his Christianity in broad terms."

I tried to beg off politely. But she said it was too late to find a replacement. I decided I'd take the matter up with the professor and the publisher. Surely they'd see reason and change the theme or bend it to conform with reality. But an hour passed, then another, and the panelists still hadn't shown up. "I guess they're not coming," the producer said with amazing equanimity.

"But what about your show?"

"It doesn't matter. This was just a preliminary meeting. We'll shoot it tomorrow at eleven A.M."

Next morning, I set out for RAI a lot less ebulliently than the day before. It wasn't just the encounter with the producer that had deflated my spirits and self-esteem. The water in my neighborhood had mysteriously been shut off, and I had had to bathe and shave with a bottle of heated Ferrarelle. Then a massive student demonstration blocked the center of the city, and I had to walk a mile to reach a functioning bus line. I arrived a half hour late, and the producer, professor, and publisher were already at the studio. Or rather, they were clustered outside the locked door to the studio. Neither the technical crew nor Mila Vannucci had checked in.

We waited for over an hour, debating about Christianity and Henry James, American versus Italian efficiency, and crime in the streets. I asked the publisher about the authors on his list. He said he didn't publish authors. He published encyclopedias. It was unclear why he had been brought down from Turin to discuss Henry James.

After waiting a second hour, we went to a nearby trattoria

for lunch. I assumed RAI would pick up the tab. I assumed wrong. But, after all, I was going to be well paid for a few minutes' work—if, that is, we ever got around to it.

We strolled back to the studio at 3 P.M. The technical crew was there now and they were irate. They'd been waiting since two-thirty. The producer snapped that we had been waiting since eleven-thirty. A harried assistant shuffling a sheaf of papers took me aside and said there was a slight bureaucratic problem about paying foreigners. These things couldn't be done quickly in Italy. I certainly couldn't expect to be paid today. He doubted I'd be paid that month.

"What about this year?" I said as a joke.

"There's a good chance," he said, dead serious, "you'll never be paid. It's so complicated."

Before I could ask more questions I was called onto the set. Mila Vannucci had arrived and was eager to get on with the show. I took my seat, stomach churning with anger and impatience and too much wine at lunch. After light checks and sound tests, we were ready to start at three-thirty. The professor opened with an introduction, attempting to place James in the context of American literature. He compared James to somebody named Harry Melville, and the producer shouted, "Cut! It's Hair-mon Melville, not Harry."

We reshot the intro, and now Mila Vannucci shouted, "Cut!" She didn't like the lighting. It was all wrong, she screamed *alta voce*. "I've been in this business thirty years. This is my life." She stalked off the set and refused to return until she had changed her makeup to compensate for the glare. We reshot the intro a third time, and just when I thought we'd finally begin the discussion, the professor announced that RAI had assembled some film footage that he was sure viewers would enjoy. Members of the panel were advised to watch the monitor.

While a narrator filled in the barest details of James's biography, the monitor showed a tape that had, at best, a tenuous connection with the author's life. True, there were photographs of the artist as a young man and of Rome during his first trip here in 1869. But the rest of the clip resembled something cobbled together for a Monty Python skit. There were shots of jazz age flappers dancing the Charleston, of champagne flowing in speakeasies and Ford flivvers trundling down Fifth Avenue. There were shots of cheerleaders and drum majorettes, Louis Armstrong playing the trumpet, a gleaming 1953 Studebaker, and, just as the narrator ended with James's death in 1916, an overhead view of the Macy's Thanksgiving Day parade, featuring dozens of inflated Walt Disney creatures. With visions of Donald Duck dancing on his retinas, the professor asked me how Henry James was regarded in America.

"I'll tell you this," I answered after a long, stunned pause. "He's never been regarded as a member of the jazz age, and no one ever connected him with Macy's Thanksgiving Day parade. I'm afraid this film may confuse an Italian audience."

"Cut!" The producer demanded to know what I had against the film clip. With great effort, I explained that there was no possible equation between James's prose and Louis Armstrong's music. "Well," she said, "it doesn't matter. We'll edit the material."

"Before six-thirty?" I asked, incredulous.

"This program won't be broadcast tonight. It'll be another month or two. Let's start the discussion again."

Once the cameras were rolling, the professor asked me to discuss Christian influences on James—precisely what I had told him I didn't care to discuss. But at this point, I would have said Henry James was the Pope if it would have gotten me out of the studio. I mumbled something about his fiction demonstrating Kant's assertion that the worst sin is to treat people as means rather than ends.

The encyclopedia publisher carried the conversation from there, observing that James's work was full of descriptions of churches. Mila Vannucci admitted she was ill-equipped to comment on the subject, but having once acted in a stage version of *Washington Square,* she said she had sensed deep spiritual vibrations. That seemed to settle the matter and serve as a transition to her dramatic reading.

First, however, there was another break so that she could rehearse. By the time she was ready, the rest of us, who wore no makeup, gleamed with sweat under the lights, and I was filled with a fierce longing for those brisk, superficial American talk shows where guests are bustled on and off every five minutes. But I figured this couldn't last much longer.

Speaking slowly, enunciating each syllable, reading with great feeling, Miss Vannucci became so caught up in her performance she did not realize she was rattling pages against the microphone. The producer called, "Cut!" This break dragged on for twenty minutes as technicians tried to resynchronize some recorded mood music with Miss Vannucci's voice.

When her reading ended, I revived from the heat and torpor, anxious to race outside, catch a taxi home, take a long cool bath, and fix an even longer, cooler drink. But no, we still weren't finished. The producer insisted on shooting reaction and establishing shots.

It was nearly six-thirty by the time our torment ended. It had taken three hours to shoot sixteen minutes of film and to watch a fourteen-minute clip of Henry James and a 1953 Studebaker. I had wasted an entire day—two days, if you counted yesterday—and I harbored no delusions I'd ever be paid.

Outside, rush-hour traffic thundered beside the Tiber. Buses were full, and there were no taxis. Impatient, I wound up walking to my apartment, wondering where Pia Zadora was at this moment. I thought of the invincibly cheerful author of *How to Teach Your Cat to Smile.* Surely she would have some upbeat advice for an exhausted and outraged fellow writer.

Six weeks later, when RAI broadcast the program, I was pleased to see that only one drum majorette and a distant shot of flivvers on Fifth Avenue remained as puzzling visual aids to the narrated biography. I was considerably less pleased that the translator who was supposed to render my pearls of wisdom into perfect Italian had been given a script and instructed to read it over my voice with little regard for what I had said. In the final frames, as if aghast at what was being done to me, I moved my mouth, but no sound came out. I sat there silently sputtering while Mila Vannucci looked on with a serene smile, sensing deep spiritual vibrations.

• • • • •

TUSCANY, ROOMS, AND VIEWS

To sit on a terrace in Tuscany with a glass of Chianti Classico in hand is to experience a sense of longing that has beset foreigners for centuries. One wants somehow to capture and preserve the essence of the place. Generations of artists, among them the greatest painters in history, have immortalized the countryside with its soft undulating hills, its cypress and olive trees. Lyrical poets have praised its lambent beauty and golden light. Pop singers and tourist brochures have, in more literal language, extolled the province's palpable charms and urged visitors to reach out and touch someone or something—if not a bronze body at Porto Ercole, then a pair of Gucci boots in Florence.

Some people, not fully satisfied with a tour of the vineyards, a few afternoons in the Uffizi, and a suitcase of souvenirs, decide they want a permanent stake and they buy property in Tuscany. In effect, they attempt to enter a work of art and live their lives in cadence with those lyrical poems and popular songs. What they find, in fact, is a world less romantic and harmonious, but fortunately more humorous and fascinating than they would have imagined. To appreciate this humor and fascination, however, one needs ample patience, an enterprising lawyer, and some basic background information.

Donald Stewart has lived in Italy almost twenty years. A consultant to various international magazines, he is also a writer and has published a novel and a number of short stories and poems in the *New Yorker*. He is currently finishing a memoir about his father, Donald Ogden Stewart, a playwright, humorist, and screenwriter best known for his Academy Award–winning script for *The Philadelphia Story*. But Stewart frequently finds his work schedule interrupted by panicky calls from American friends who have taken the plunge and purchased real estate here. Because he is married to an Italian and knows Tuscany well, especially the towns along the coast, he has served as a friendly ear, father confessor, and, all too often, a psychotherapist for people who suddenly discover they own a house without water or an apartment in a building that is about to be condemned.

In Stewart's experience, the most common mistake made by foreigners is to buy property for which no clear title exists. In a country where for centuries the records in small villages and rural areas were casually kept by the parish priest, and where family relationships are complicated, it is always difficult to establish who owns that rustic farmhouse or ruined stable that could so easily be converted into a vacation cottage.

Seduced by low prices and less than candid salesmen, Americans will sometimes sign a contract to purchase a house from a local farmer named, let's say, Domenico Domenici. Months or even years later, once the house has been paid for and renovated from the foundation to the roof beams, a simple shepherd will show up, introduce himself, and inform the foreign interlopers that his name is Domenico Domenici too and he has a claim on the place equal to his cousin's, the other Domenico Domenici. To prove his case, he will produce a blurry photocopy of some ancient document now moldering in a church rectory.

Of course, if the new owners don't care to be reasonable, they can always take the case to court. But the legal proceedings will last for a decade, the lawyers' fees will amount to millions of lire, and the trial, when it finally transpires, will bear a closer resemblance to *La Traviata* than to *Perry Mason*. Why endure a long, knock-down, dragged-out legal battle—Verbose Encounters of the Absurd Kind, Donald Stewart calls them—when one can simply pay the second (then perhaps a third and fourth) Domenico Domenici a few thousand dollars to abandon his claim on the house.

Like the Ancient Mariner, Stewart tells a tale full of wonderment and woe about an acquaintance who had no trouble with his Tuscan country home until twenty years after the sale, when he himself decided to sell it. A businessman from Turin wanted to buy the place, but he was a methodical sort, well versed in the Byzantine intricacies of Italian real estate and preternaturally alert to the legal problems a truly creative mind can conjure up in this country.

First, the prospective buyer insisted on a title search that went back for generations and, sure enough, he discovered a couple of anomalies. In the contract signed by the current American owner, the house and surrounding property were described with meticulous precision. But two details listed on previous contracts for the house had not made it onto the present deed. Every room was mentioned—except a second-floor bedroom which, fifty years ago, had been willed in perpetuity to the previous owner's brother and his heirs. In the yard out front, the fruit of a peach tree had been bequeathed to a cousin. The businessman from Turin refused to buy the place—in fact, he explained, anybody would be a fool to buy it—until these potential points of litigation were resolved.

The American assumed it would be easy to settle the matter of the peach tree. The woman who owned the fruit had not claimed it for the past two decades and she was now quite old.

The upstairs bedroom was a dicier situation. For one thing, the people who supposedly owned it had moved out of the area and might prove hard to trace. For another thing, the room no longer existed. The American had opened that end of the house and built a terrace.

As so often in Italy, reality has a habit of reversing one's expectations. The American quickly located the owners of the upstairs bedroom and they were terribly accommodating. They had no wish to occupy their property and they did not care to punish anyone for destroying it. For a mere $2,000, they would sign away all their present and future rights to the now nonexistent room.

But the woman who owned the peaches proved to be far more difficult to deal with. Although she was half blind and too crippled to pick fruit from her tree, she revealed that she had a son who lived in a nearby city and he and his children had expressed a keen interest in reclaiming their patrimony. She herself was more than willing to relinquish her rights, but she had to consider her family and their wishes.

Their wishes, expressed during negotiations of a length and complexity comparable to the SALT talks, were quite vociferous. They wanted $10,000. If they didn't get it, they intended to camp around that tree in front of the American's house from the instant the first blossom appeared every spring until they harvested the final peach every fall. In the end, they compromised, and the American paid them $7,500.

"You'd think that would clear the way for the fellow to close the deal with the businessman from Turin," Donald Stewart says. "But there was still the question of the horses in the field."

A few years back, a local farmer had asked the American if he could graze his horses on a few acres of unused land. Figuring that this would save him the trouble of mowing that

125

field, the American had agreed. No documents were signed; no rent was paid by the farmer. It was just a neighborly arrangement. The farmer fenced in the field, herded his horses onto the grassy pasture during the summer, and led them elsewhere in winter.

But when the American wanted to sell the property, the farmer politely informed him that the field didn't belong to him anymore. It now belonged to the farmer because he had "improved" the piece of "abandoned" land. He would, however, do the decent thing and stand aside—if the American would pay him $35,000.

This dispute is still in court, where it is likely to remain until the end of the century. It turned out that the farmer has pulled this scam five other times on foreigners and figures to die a rich man if a couple of his claims are upheld by the magistrate.

By separating the field from the rest of his property, the American finally managed to sell the house and the land surrounding it. But the story does not end there. As Donald Stewart points out, repatriating a cliché to its country of origin, "The opera ain't over until the fat lady sings," and in Italy, no business deal is finished until the final suit has been filed. In this case, a real estate agent whom neither the American nor the businessman from Turin had ever met has claimed that she initiated, negotiated, and executed the agreement between the buyer and seller, and therefore has a legal right to 4 percent of the price.

If this all sounds like a version of *Catch 22* as written in a collaborative effort by Franz Kafka and the Marquis de Sade, it must be remembered that the quirks and eccentricities of buying property in Tuscany—and elsewhere in Italy, for that matter—are more than matched by the challenges of renovating a villa, then actually living in it. Fifteen years ago, Robert and Beverly Katz bought a house in a small town outside of Arezzo. They lived in Rome, where Katz worked as a novelist—*Cassandra Crossing*—and an investigative journalist—*Days of Wrath*, a book about Aldo Moro's kidnapping and assassination that caused considerable controversy when it was recently made into the movie *Il Caso Moro*. But the Katzes wanted a place in the country where they could go with their two sons on weekends and vacations.

They found a spot that was at that time so undeveloped the villagers thought the Katzes were crazy to move to a remote area just when the local people were flocking to Rome, Florence, and Milan. The natives also couldn't quite get a handle on what the Katzes intended to do with a ruined farmhouse. Why, for example, did they want to tear out the stalls and the warren of small rooms on the ground floor where the previous owner had kept his animals?

When Katz explained that he was an American, and he and his wife wanted to install some modern conveniences inside the beautiful shell of the original structure, the workers he hired said they would draw up plans that coincided with his wishes. They came back with a blueprint that included an escalator from the ground floor to the second story and a revolving door at the front entrance. This, they said, was modern and American.

Katz thanked them, but explained that he preferred a wooden staircase. The front door was fine as it stood.

Years later, when he decided to build a swimming pool, Katz learned that he would need two things: an expert with dynamite and an official *permesso di lavoro*, or building permit. People warned him it would take years to obtain a legal permit. It was better to go ahead and put in his pool and count on the authorities to give him retroactive permission. As for a demolition expert, there was no need to pay for one when a local man had all the skills necessary to blast a hole in the stony ground behind the house.

"I had my doubts, though," Katz admits, "when the guy showed up with a box of dynamite. I noticed right away he had only three fingers on one hand."

In fact, the blaster worked out well. It was the building permit that nearly cost Katz a couple of his own fingers as he gnawed them impatiently waiting for the *permesso* to be

127

granted. With this experience, he mastered a basic truth about life in Italy: "There is always the legal and the illegal way of doing things. The legal way is invariably a lot longer, much more trouble, and ultimately more expensive. It's better to go ahead and do what you want and be prepared to pay a lawyer and a fine later."

Like Donald Stewart, Katz acknowledges the difficulties of buying and maintaining a country property in Tuscany, but believes it's worth the price in money, time, and emotional damage. "Where else could a Jewish boy from Brooklyn have his own vineyard and his own label? And where else could he pick up such bizarre stories? The first time I wanted to take a few bottles of my wine back to the States, people in the village warned me not to. They said it was absolutely impossible. I thought it was another lunatic law they have here. Like you can't transport your own wine without a license. But no, what they meant is the moon was in the wrong position. If I moved it, I'd ruin it."

Did he take their warning to heart?

"These days I do things strictly *all'italiana*," Katz said. "I mean, I'm not about to have a revolving door on my house. But to survive here you have to listen and learn."

◆ ◆ ◆ ◆ ◆

CASH, DON'T LEAVE HOME WITHOUT IT

When it comes to banking, finance, and credit, Italy regards with great suspicion many basic assumptions shared by developed nations throughout the world. Unless a newcomer grasps the quirky fiscal principles here, he cannot possibly comprehend the country or, for that matter, hope to handle the most rudimentary business transactions. To pay a bill, open a bank account, or cash a check, Americans in particular must suspend their cherished notions of logic and convenience.

While the United States has evolved into something close to a cashless society in which an enormous amount of buying and selling takes place via charge cards and computers, Italy remains immured in an age where cash is king and confidential deals are commonplace. Of course, credit cards exist, but fewer than 4 percent of Italians, as opposed to 75 percent of American families, own a piece of plastic. Checking accounts also exist, but there's little point in opening one, since personal checks are about as acceptable as five-day-old fish. Even the nationalized utility companies demand cash.

Thus it is that every two months, when the gas, electricity, and telephone bills arrive, the population moves en masse, like an immense nomadic tribe, its pockets bulging with billions of lire that must be paid out at local post offices, which insist on exacting a fee for allowing one the privilege of standing in line for hours, then forking over fistfuls of money.

Any suggestion that this bimonthly baptism of fire could be avoided by the simple expedient of permitting customers to pay bills by sending checks through the mail is greeted with rude noises and cryptic obscene gestures. As nobody knows better than postal employees, the mail is undependable. In fact, a fellow has to count himself lucky if all of his ten-thousand-, fifty-thousand-, and hundred-thousand-lire bills are accepted as legal tender. A lot of the currency here looks and feels and sometimes smells as if it has served strange purposes. As film director Billy Wilder once mused, "What kind of country is it where you can't tear the toilet paper, but the money falls apart in your hands?"

Given the fact that most Italian banks harbor grave misgivings about checks—even their own checks!—one cannot really blame others for refusing to honor them. Just recently I had occasion to receive a check from the London *Sunday Times,* drafted in lire on their own account at a Roman bank. When I carried it there to be cashed, the teller informed me it would take three weeks for the check to clear.

Clear what? I asked. It could be withdrawn directly from the *Times* account. If the bank had any doubts, it could cable or call the *Times* for confirmation. But no, that was impossible, the teller informed me. He had to follow the proper procedure.

What he meant, I finally inferred, is that he had to protect the *Times* against itself. How could he be sure that it hadn't made a rash mistake in issuing me a check? Maybe the *Times* would regret it later and want it back. At the very least, as long as he delayed, the money would remain in his client's account. He saw no advantage in paying me until he absolutely had to.

Whereas American banks have become action-oriented, full-service facilities where one can save, invest, borrow, or finance anything from a pickup truck to a leveraged buy-out of a multinational conglomerate, Italian banks regard themselves essentially as religious organizations, as heirs to those contemplative monastic orders which preserved secret rituals and classical knowledge during the Dark Ages. Just like those ancient monks who protected precious manuscripts and spent years copying them by hand, the tellers of today view their primary mission as spiritual. Sure, they offer a safe place for valuables, but their abiding interest is in values, such as thrift, patience, discipline, and fiscal conservatism.

To enter an institution such as the Banco di Santo Spirito (Bank of the Holy Ghost) is to submit oneself to a catechism class conducted in a slow antiphonal chorus. Express lines, curb service, drive-through windows—these fiendish offenses against the natural law are absent. Since the deepest obligation here is to eternal verities, not to transient customers, potential converts are expected to prove their faith by opening an account with a minimum deposit of $25,000. Afterward, they will have ample opportunity to demonstrate that they accept the evidence of things unseen. Many Italian banks send out statements only twice a year, which makes balancing one's books a little like living in fear and trembling. When one does bounce a check, punishment is swift and severe. It's not uncommon to be charged a penalty equal to 30 percent of an overdraft.

Under the circumstances, it isn't surprising that many sinners prefer to keep their money under their mattresses. This provides quick access to cash and offers the additional advantage of not leaving a paper trail that can be followed by tax collectors or suspicious spouses who might notice a canceled check or credit-card stub and question that puzzling hotel bill or two-hundred-dollar meal in Milan. But this definitely has a downside for anybody who needs a receipt or some proof of purchase, for that unlucky individual must, in effect, pay a surcharge on goods and services for which he has already paid in full.

For example, the annual income generated by real estate transactions in Italy is underreported by an estimated 42 percent, and it is extremely difficult for a tenant to get anything in writing from a landlord. If one absolutely insists on a receipt, the landlord is apt to raise the rent to cover the taxes he was trying to evade. Thus a $1,000-a-month apartment balloons to $1,500.

Similar increases can occur in restaurants and shops when one indicates one intends to pay with a credit card. Suddenly realizing that there will be a record of the transaction, the waiter or clerk scurries off, and the owner appears and explains that somehow someone somewhere forgot to include the 20-percent value-added tax in the bill. But, of course, if the customer pays cash, then he can avoid the extra charge and inconvenience.

The same dizzying tarantella takes place here almost every time money changes hands, and this catches foreigners, especially Americans, by surprise. They might expect and even enjoy a marathon bargaining session in an Arab bazaar. But they find it less amusing in Italy to spend hours hammering out an agreement about a price, only to discover that they then have to start haggling over whether there will be an honest record of the deal.

Having lived in Rome for so many years, I know better than to waste energy asking a plumber, a maid, or a mechanic for a receipt. But I confess I am still occasionally left dumbstruck by the size and complexity of the financial arrangements which local entrepreneurs suggest should be conducted under the table.

My sons attend a well-known international school whose student body is composed largely of the children of diplomats and corporate executives from many nations. If people from such diverse backgrounds can be said to share any common denominator, it is a daunting savoir faire and a formidable talent at negotiating agreements. This past fall, a number of them worked along with school officials to arrange daily transportation for the students. After soliciting opinions, taking bids, and even entertaining the idea of hiring a fleet of taxis, they decided to bestow their patronage on a private bus company which had a reputation for dependable service and reasonable prices. The only problem was that this reputable, reasonable, and dependable bus company wanted to charge approximately $100,000 a year, yet it refused to sign a contract or to give a receipt.

Frankly, few parents were shocked that the company intended to commit tax fraud on such a grand scale. Cosmopolitan to the core, they chalked this up to cultural differences and drew no invidious conclusions. But some of the corporate executives and embassy personnel demanded that the deal be killed. It seems that their respective firms and governments would not reimburse them for money spent on their children's education unless they could supply documentation. So the kids are now being delivered to school by a flotilla of buses that cost considerably more and arrive and depart on a haphazard schedule that varies as much as two hours a day. But at least the company provides prompt receipts.

The same cannot be said for one of our family doctors. My younger boy has allergies, and for years we took him to a specialist who is reputed to be the best in Rome. After months of dishing up lame excuses, then lying outright and claiming that it is against the law to give a foreigner a receipt —in fact, the law is precisely the opposite—the feckless physician came clean and admitted he didn't want any record of our dealings that might fall into the hands of the tax auditors. He wouldn't even sign an American insurance form that would have allowed us to recoup part of our costs.

With some minor lingering dyspepsia, I was willing to swallow this indignity. After all, I reasoned, my boy was getting excellent medical attention even if I wasn't getting a receipt. But then I found out that the doctor's determination to avoid taxes was so all-consuming, he had failed to keep a file on our son's case. On every visit, we had to remind him of his previous diagnosis and tell him which medication he had prescribed. We might as well have submitted the boy to the ministrations of a forgetful faith healer.

We have now switched to the second-best specialist in town. He's a diligent doctor and an easygoing tax evader. Although he, too, refuses to give receipts, he signs the American insurance forms with theatrical indifference, shrugging, as if to suggest, "They'll never take me alive." Or perhaps he just can't place much importance in a document which, unlike those in Italy, doesn't come emblazoned with official stamps and notarized seals.

This cavalier attitude sometimes characterizes Italian art dealers, who are surprisingly willing to supply elaborate documentation for work bought by tourists. I recently heard of a case in which one of my fellow countrymen purchased an expensive Renaissance Madonna. Naturally, he demanded a receipt and written certification of the painting's provenance.

After a brief dispute, the dealer agreed to assemble the necessary information and have it ready the day before the customer flew back to the States. At the appointed hour he arrived at the hotel carrying a thick sheaf of papers. The American reviewed them and discovered two complete sets of documents. The first contained an accurate account of what had been paid for the painting and an impressive array of evidence attesting to its bona fides. The second set listed a much lower price and contained testimony from art critics and historians who swore that the painting was merely a modern imitation of an ancient masterpiece.

The American insisted on an immediate explanation, which the imperturbable Italian was more than willing to provide. The first receipt and set of documents, he said, were valid and they satisfied the customer's requirements for proof. The second receipt and documents were false and were meant to hoodwink Italian authorities, who, as the American should know, would never allow a real Renaissance masterpiece to leave the country without the approval of the Belle Arti commission. Such approval, the art dealer pointed out, would take years and cost thousands of dollars. It was so much wiser and simpler to use the bogus second set of documents to clear customs in Rome and avoid duty in New York.

"But how can I be sure what's true and what's false?" the American demanded.

The response, I like to imagine, was the same monumental shrug I see whenever my son's devil-may-care allergist scrawls his indecipherable signature on an insurance form.

• • • • •

WINTER ON THE RIVIERA

Some destinations strike a traveler with all the heart-stopping force of love at first sight. But remarkably, for me, the Riviera was not such a spot. My initial reaction was one of deep disappointment every bit as unreasonable as the heavy freight of romantic expectations that had carried me there. The Côte d'Azur, the coast between Saint-Tropez and the Italian border, simply didn't measure up to my wild imaginings, which had been prompted by repeated readings of F. Scott Fitzgerald's *Tender Is the Night* and long exposure to literary anecdotes about Gerald and Sara Murphy's hospitality at Villa America on Cap d'Antibes.

There were, I should add, extenuating circumstances. Before setting off from Paris, I had reached out to keep a métro door from slamming and had somehow wound up sticking my hand straight through the window. The cut on my wrist required twenty-six stitches and a triple-strength tetanus shot that left me feverish and addled on the drive through southern France.

To add to my misery, we were traveling in early November, and the weather was cold, blustery, and wet. When we reached the Riviera, a leaden rain falling from a low sky ruined the views of famous hotel façades, pastel villas, and fabled beaches with names like Tahiti, La Garoupe, and Baie des Anges. But since my dream vision of the Côte d'Azur did not allow for the existence of anything so unpleasant as winter, I refused to accept the evidence of my senses and swallowed the assurances of a local real estate agent who swore to my wife and me that this freakish spell of evil weather would soon end, and the sun-drenched beaches would be carpeted with bronzed bodies. Meanwhile, he urged us to take advantage of low-season rates and rent a cottage in the countryside behind Cannes. The living-room fireplace would be adequate, he said, to heat the house on rare chilly mornings and evenings.

With a grant from the Fulbright Commission—the annual stipend was $2,700—I had moved to France to finish a novel, but I spent more time that winter chopping wood than writing, and the highest expression of my artistry went into building fires, not crafting prose. Even so, we nearly froze to death, especially during December, when for a week the rain turned to snow. Yet, in retrospect, I believe that every early setback could ultimately be viewed as . . . well, if not a pleasure, at least an educational experience.

My sliced-up hand, for example, had to be unstitched, and the doctor who did this not only dramatized certain basic differences between American and French medical practices —he offered me a glass of cognac as an anesthetic—he choreographed my lone literary encounter of the year. Explaining that one of his patients was the world's most famous novelist, he introduced me to Harold Robbins, who lived in Le Cannet and generously shared with me the secret of his success. "Remember, kid," he advised me over drinks at the Carlton Hotel, "you can't sell a million copies unless they print a million books." For the past twenty years, I have attempted to live by this self-evident truth, which is no less valid just because my publishers have adamantly refused to recognize its wisdom.

Because of our acute discomfort indoors, we were reduced to spending hours every day in our Volkswagen, which offered the only sure source of warmth available to us. Cruising through the countryside with the heater turned on full force, we admitted that this really was an extraordinarily lovely and interesting corner of the world, and we came to know it very well from these daily life-sustaining drives.

I don't mean to suggest that we saw everything from a hurtling, well-heated car, nor do I want to leave the impression that the Côte d'Azur has the same climate as Antarctica. In fact, its winters rather resemble those of, let's say, Little Rock, Arkansas: mild for the most part, a bit rainy, occasionally very cold when the wind blows out of the north, quite balmy when it comes from the south. It is not to be mistaken for the Caribbean—the temperature seldom rises above the low sixties between December and April—but the Riviera is ideal for walking, and we covered much of it on foot. While it would be foolish to claim that in such a well-known and often-written-about region we discovered anything new, we nevertheless had the pleasure of feeling and savoring the sensations described by earlier travelers.

Canopied by palms, we walked the length of La Croisette in Cannes, where the shops along the waterfront looked as if their display windows had been laid out and lighted for aesthetic, rather than strictly commercial, purposes. Like connoisseurs in a museum, we strolled past an all but unbroken tapestry of silk ties and designer gowns, costly leather coats, purses, and shoes.

We explored the pine-shaded and pine-scented peninsulas of Cap Martin, Cap d'Antibes, and Cap Ferrat, and hiked through olive groves and forests of tall, flame-shaped cypress trees. In February we saw the hillsides blaze with acid-yellow mimosas, and we watched the mistral bring down a blizzard of pink almond blossoms. We toured perfume factories in the town of Grasse and ceramic shops in Vallauris, botanical gardens in Eze, and the picturesque little fishing port in Villefranche, where it must have been decades since a real fisherman had docked his boat. We climbed the ramparts of ancient towns that had repulsed hordes of invaders but had fallen victims to tourism, and we ate in a restaurant where, legend has it, Zelda Fitzgerald flung herself down a flight of stairs to get Scott's attention. We visited the Léger museum, the Picasso museum, and the Matisse chapel, a surprisingly small room with white tile walls that looked as though they had been decorated by a very talented child with a black felt-tip pen. Much more to my liking was the Fondation Maeght, just outside of Saint-Paul de Vence, where a permanent collection of sculpture by Mirò, Giacometti, and Calder is on display in the garden while a rotating schedule of shows takes place inside.

Monte Carlo, I admit, was a disappointment. With so many high-rise condos and office buildings crowded around the harbor, the tiny principality struck me as a mouth stuffed with too many false teeth. Still, there were the Grimaldi family's fairy-book castle and Jacques Cousteau's aquarium.

By contrast, Nice was a real city, bristling with life and surprises. La Promenade des Anglais, a broad avenue curving around the bay, might give Nice the appearance of just another wealthy, well-manicured resort, but a few short steps away from the pebble-strewn beach lies the *ancienne ville,* the old area of town, and there the atmosphere is more raffish than resort-like, and the crumbling, close-set buildings seem to lean against each other for support. Unlike the frothy white confection of the hotels along the waterfront, the houses here are painted in earth tones of ocher, terracotta, and burnt sienna, and the narrow streets and piazzas are thronged with people speaking the local patois. On Cours Saleya, an open-air market offers an abundance of produce which, like the boutique windows in Cannes, appears to have been laid out by artists, not merchants. I remember immense pyramids of oranges and lemons, giant corsages of zucchini flowers, braids of garlic bulbs, vats of olives bobbing in brine, aromatic arrangements of lavender, thyme, and rosemary.

The marketplace invariably made us hungry and we would often stop at some nameless hole-in-the-wall restaurant and have a bowl of *soupe au pistou* or a fish broth afloat with large croutons covered with a garlic paste called *rouille.* Or else we would grab a snack—a *pan bagnat,* a sandwich of *salade niçoise* on a bun, or a slice of *pissaladière,* a sort of onion tart—and keep on walking and looking.

One of my favorite spots in Nice is the Lawn Tennis Club, which is nestled among the shrubs of the Parc Impériale. Even when no match is in progress, there is plenty to see from the bleacher seats on center court. The surrounding hills provide examples of every architectural style that has had a season of popularity over the past century. Turning a full 360 degrees, one notices turreted castles with barred windows, gun slots, and steep slate roofs; the glistening spires and onion domes of the Russian Orthodox church; whitewashed North African façades with crenellated towers and keyhole arches; cubistic villas painted salmon-pink or burnt orange; Art Deco mansions, their sleek lines reiterated by iron railings; and finally, enormous modern slablike apartment houses. For hours I have sat at the Tennis Club, drugged by sunlight, dizzied by the scent of flowers, Gauloises Bleus, and the distant sea, thinking, This is enough. I don't need to move from here. This is the pure essence of the south of France.

But eventually we found other out-of-the-way places on the Riviera that we liked even more. We were especially enamored of the *villages perchés*— perched villages—which lay like a necklace of jewels about ten miles inland on a line from the Italian border to Marseilles. While many of them had been discovered, tidied up, and transformed into chic vacation flats long before our arrival, others still had the look and feel of isolated medieval towns. To stroll through their empty cobblestone streets on a winter afternoon was to enter a time warp, to feel one had been carried back to an age when people cowered behind high walls, clinging for safety to a church and a castle. But, of course, even in the least developed villages there was an occasional TV antenna or the metallic *ack-ack* of a pinball machine in a café to break the illusion.

Yet although this illusion, along with so many of our other romantic pipe dreams about the Riviera, was shattered, the spell of the place held. It still holds now, twenty years later. Having been back many times during the summer, I don't regret that we happened to spend our first months there in winter when we had the coast more or less to ourselves and could travel anywhere without fear of traffic jams and tourist gridlock. We were even lucky, I continue to try to convince myself, to have rented that hideously cold house. Otherwise, we might have huddled indoors and missed so much.

As a French friend expressed it with an admirable Gallic earthiness and a sense of aphorism: "To see France in the summer when all the trees are in leaf and to claim that you love it is like looking at a woman with her clothes on. You might imagine that you love her. But you'll never know until you see the truth. Winter is when you see this country's bare bones. If you learn to love it then, you'll make a lasting marriage."

• • • • •

GORE VIDAL: PURITAN
MORALIST

We all know Gore Vidal. Or imagine we do. How could we not? More often quoted than many political candidates, more frequently interviewed than any actor or rock star, a habitué of the late-night talk shows which shape the public consciousness at its most elemental level, Vidal is one of a few serious writers whose names are recognized in Europe as well as the United States. Even people who have never bought a book—especially people who have never bought a book—express vehement opinions about him.

Yet in spite of the perfervid emotions he provokes, and in spite of his apparent ubiquity, Gore Vidal has divulged little about himself. If he ever experiences doubt or indulges in self-pity, it is not with interviewers. Perhaps there are occasions when he discusses secrets from his past or reveals his innermost self, but he doesn't do so on talk shows.

A certain remote and impersonal—not to mention imperious—attitude may be integral to Vidal's psychology. But he has accentuated this detachment for professional reasons. As he admits in one of his essays, he refuses to use himself as a subject of analysis either in interviews or in his fiction on the "ground that since we live in a time where the personality of the writer is everything and what he writes is nothing, only a fool would aid the enemy by helping to trivialize his works."

However, such aloofness can be dangerous. While Vidal insists like some biblical prophet that only by his works shall ye know him, he realizes that a radically different scale of values guides most literary critics. To them, "what matters is not if a book is good or bad (who, after all, would know the difference?) but whether or not the author is a good person or a bad person." Thus, since Vidal's character has always been suspect, his reputation as an artist has suffered, and much as he may call for attention to his work, far more attention will focus on him.

Commercially this has been to his advantage. For he learned early that although he couldn't control what reviewers said, he was a talented self-publicist and could sell books. The result: millions of dollars in royalties, which rose in value when he converted them into Swiss francs and deutsch marks—as a protest against the war in Vietnam, he claims. ("Civic virtue can be surprisingly rewarding.") He owns a house in Los Angeles, and he rents a penthouse apartment in Rome and a villa overlooking the Amalfi coast.

Critically, however, Vidal has ridden a dizzying roller coaster, having been called "our greatest living man of letters" just about as often as he has suffered personal attacks as "a bad piece of work." There is no doubt that his image has done much of the damage, confusing some readers, infuriating others. In a supposedly democratic age, he has played the contemptuous patrician. During his frequent public appearances, he has come across as altogether too wry, too acerbic and glib—suspicious behavior in the eyes of those Book Chat writers who value earnestness over everything. When the vogue was for two-fisted writers of irreproachable masculinity, he said he was, "like everyone else," bisexual. When fashion changed and homosexuality might have been in Vidal's favor, he still said he was bisexual. But perhaps worst of all, he made his most difficult achievements look easy. And he had the temerity to put his finger on why he is so often resented. "Americans prefer their serious writers obscure, poor, and, if possible, doomed by drink or gaudy vice"—all the things which Vidal is not.

One might expect more perspicacious critics to make a distinction between Vidal's image and work, between the public's notions about him and what he actually produces. But even in the recent *Harvard Guide to Contemporary American Writing* there are indications that authors are judged as much by their personae as by their books. While granting that Vidal's career "has embodied perhaps the most concerted effort of any postwar novelist to establish himself as a 'man of letters' on the European model, equally at home in a variety of forms," the *Guide* remarks that his "hothouse beginning may have caused his public self-creation to lag somewhat behind the creation of his works. In that interaction between working author and public person that Mailer has made so central to his career, Vidal works with a certain clumsiness and ineptness, his mandarin narcissism an intriguing contrast to Mailer's struggling self-obsession."

A curious comment, indeed. In his eagerness to catalogue what he takes to be Vidal's flaws as a performer, the critic has overlooked certain inconvenient facts. For instance, after high school Vidal enlisted in the Army as a private; Mailer went to Harvard—speaking of hothouse beginnings.

But then, perhaps the critic shouldn't be blamed. As already mentioned, few people know much about Gore Vidal.

His house in Los Angeles, a huge, whitewashed Spanish Provincial, stands behind a screen of foliage in a canyon in the Hollywood Hills. Vidal answered the door and led me through a dim hallway into the living room, which is brightened by red walls and many windows. Obviously done by a decorator, the room is a collision of Andalucia and the

Orient. There are Moorish arches and banquettes, a Persian carpet, a rattan coffee table, a Japanese screen. The books and magazines scattered about—*The Nation,* William Golding's novel *Darkness Visible, An Illustrated History of the Civil War, Jerry Brown Illustrated,* a book of photos about China, a thick volume entitled *L'Amour bleu*—are as eclectic as the décor and seem to mark the outermost limits of Vidal's wide-ranging interests.

"Let me give you the tour," he said.

"The tour" consisted of a stroll through the yard, not through the house. He pointed out a patio where the swimming pool had once been. The new one was up a flight of steps, on a terrace. As we stood beside it, gazing at the red tile roof of the house, Vidal remarked that it reminded him of the setting of a Raymond Chandler mystery.

Although many assume that he spends most of his time in Italy, Vidal has always returned to America for promotional tours, and as co-chairman with Dr. Spock of the People's Party from 1970 till 1972, he spoke against the Vietnam War from one end of the country to the other. Since he never considered himself an expatriate—"The more I stayed abroad, the most intensely interested I became in the United States, the more clearly I saw it"—it was no great shock when in 1976, due to a change in Italian tax laws, he bought this house and began spending more than half the year outside of Italy.

By the time we returned to the living room and had settled into our chairs, we still had not made eye contact. Was it conceivable, after so many interviews, that he suffered some vestigial shyness? Or did he avert his eyes because of what he imagined he saw in mine? It cannot be pleasant to know, as all celebrities must, that interviewers are apt to take their revenge in underhanded ways, i.e., focusing on a blemish rather than a beauty mark.

Beside Vidal in the chair lay Rat, a tiny dog which bore an alarming resemblance to its name. Rat showed no reluctance to look me in the eye, and under the dog's implacable gaze I started with stock questions. When does Vidal write? Where? How?

The answers came out with crisp efficiency. In the morning. At a table. Longhand, on yellow legal pads ("just like Nixon") when he is doing fiction. Typewritten, when he's working on an essay or filmscript. He stays at it three or four hours a day and doesn't let houseguests or social commitments violate his schedule.

It is worth emphasizing that although Vidal is portrayed by his critics as a kind of *boulevardier* who goes to too many parties and knows too many famous nonliterary people, he has produced an impressive body of work in the last thirty years. Its sheer bulk—nineteen novels, a collection of short stories, five plays, four collections of essays, and numerous scripts for television and film—is all the more astounding when one considers its profusion of styles, genres, and rhetorical devices. His fiction covers the spectrum from serious, conventional realism to comic, iconoclastic surrealism. His nonfiction ranges from general assessments of literary movements to deeply moving elegies, from profiles of presidential candidates to prophetic articles about America's sexual mores, its relations with the Middle East, and its economic prognosis.

As his historical novels *Julian, Burr,* and *1876* demonstrate, Vidal is a meticulous researcher who—miracle of miracles—goes at it alone, unlike many popular novelists who hire a battalion of grad students to pillage the library stacks. Even when doing a hilarious essay such as "The Art and Arts of E. Howard Hunt," he reads the man's entire *oeuvre.* One may disagree with his opinion of the French *nouveau roman* or the American avant-garde novel, or of Yukio Mishima, Italo Calvino, or Louis Auchincloss, but one cannot deny that he has done his homework.

In short, his evenings with Paul and Joanne, Mick and Bianca (in the pre-split days), and Princess Margaret and Andy Warhol seem not to have affected the style or substance of what he writes each morning. "Why should they?" Vidal asks. "Henry James and Edith Wharton led far more active social lives and it never harmed their work." And as he takes some pleasure in repeating, an occasional dinner party couldn't possibly dry up a writer's creative juices any quicker than a steady diet of teaching freshman composition, or of circuit-riding from one campus literary conference to the next, doing the academic novelist's equivalent of a talk-show routine.

When I brought up the *Harvard Guide* and his "hothouse beginning" and "mandarin narcissism," Vidal tilted his head to one side, stared down his nose, and smiled the frosty smile he flashes on TV when he is about to take disciplinary action against a right-wing politician—in his eyes, any American politician.

"Strange," he intoned in a calm, rich voice. "I suppose I'm as egotistical as the next person. But narcissism? In what way? With the exception of *Two Sisters*, I've never drawn on my life for fiction. I sometimes talk about myself in essays, but only as a way of confessing my point of view. On television and in interviews I talk about politics or the state of the world. Frankly, I don't find it very interesting to analyze myself."

Vidal's acquaintances confirm that although he may, by sheer force of intelligence, dominate a conversation, he isn't self-absorbed. He asks questions, is surprisingly receptive to the strangers who drop in on him, and is always eager to learn something new, be it a tidbit of political gossip, the name of a rising novelist, or the symptoms of an exotic disease. (From my observation there is much discussion of medical lore *chez* Vidal.)

During TV appearances he is less likely to discuss his books than to expatiate on his current obsessions, which tend to concern the commonweal. Several years ago on the Johnny Carson show he astonished insomniacs around the country by coming on with the model of a new toilet system. It was during the long drought in California, and Vidal demonstrated how gravity-flush toilets could conserve thousands of gallons of water. It is hard to imagine any other American writer wasting precious air time when he could be plugging his work.

"As for my 'hothouse beginning,' " Vidal continued, "I guess I was born with certain advantages. But I wasn't raised in a bell jar, I wasn't pampered. I've supported myself—and others—since I was seventeen. And I didn't inherit my money, as some people think. Everything I have, I earned."

I interrupted to ask whether, considering his socialist beliefs, he felt guilty about his wealth.

"Why should I? I've never exploited anyone. I give fair value for what I get."

Still, when he received million-dollar advances, didn't that leave less for young novelists and poets?

"Well, there's no such thing as unilateral socialism. I work within the system we have . . . and it's hardly a hothouse," he circled back to the original subject. "When you look at my interests—politics, public affairs."

The phone rang. It had a row of buttons, and Vidal pressed the lighted one, then picked up the receiver. A reporter wanted his reaction to the Supreme Court decision in which novelist Gwen Davis was successfully sued by a doctor who claimed she had based an unflattering fictional character on him.

Mentioning "the chilling effect" this would have on novelists—"It'll be a nightmare. They'll have to vet every book. Does this rule out all satire?"—Vidal began to speak more precisely, anxious to be quoted correctly, breaking his words into distinct syllables, pausing at commas, stopping at periods.

The reporter inquired about Vidal's own libel suit against Truman Capote.

"That's a different matter. You simply cannot tell lies about a living person and get away with it."

The suit was prompted by Capote's story in *Playgirl* that Vidal had been thrown out of the Kennedy White House for drunkenness. Vidal has demanded an apology, exemplary damages of one dollar, and payment of his legal expenses, which amount to approximately $40,000.

While he was still speaking to the reporter, the phone rang again. Vidal said a hasty good-bye and pressed another lighted button. When a lengthy business conversation ensued, I jotted down what he was wearing. Scuffed brown shoes. Blue Lacoste socks with green alligators. Rumpled gray flannel slacks and a blue blazer.

Over the years I have seen Vidal on dozens of occasions, and he always seems to be wearing a blue blazer and rumpled gray slacks. Friends say he cares little about his personal appearance and depends on Howard Austin, his long-time companion, to advise him about clothing.

Howard claims Gore has excellent taste and prefers conservative English tailoring. It's just that he hates to shop and tends to wear the same things over and over. The first time I met Vidal at a cocktail party, he sat down and crossed his legs, revealing on the sole of one shoe a hole the size of a silver dollar. I took this as evidence that despite his reputation for narcissism, he isn't overly concerned about his image.

Not that he can't also play the Grand Man. Since his prep-school days at Exeter he has been a gifted self-dramatizer. His classmates called him the Senator, partly to mock him, partly because his grandfather, T. P. Gore, was a Senator from Oklahoma, but also in deference to Vidal's debating skill.

Then, as today, he had a reputation for being arrogant and vain. But friends say he has always had the saving grace of being able to make fun of himself. Once known as the handsomest man in Rome, he now describes himself as a classical ruin.

In fact, for a man in his mid-fifties, Vidal looks remarkably well. His hairline has receded a bit, but this has only emphasized the brainy prominence of his forehead. As his waistline waxes and wanes with the season—holiday dinner parties and lecture tours take their toll—he tries to exercise and watch his diet. Then, just before embarking on a major writing project, he goes "into training," checking into a hotel for complete privacy, giving up liquor, fasting for a few days, and generally clearing his head. "I'm no romantic," he says. "To write what I do, I have to be able to think."

After Vidal hung up, the discussion turned to his family. By now everybody knows Jacqueline Onassis and he had Hugh Auchincloss for a stepfather—at different times, it should be added. But his real father, Eugene Vidal, Sr., appears to have been a more interesting figure. A star athlete at West Point, Eugene, Sr., later returned to coach the Army football team and serve as the first instructor in aeronautics. Born in the cadet hospital, Gore was named Eugene Vidal, Jr. But then his father resigned his commission, and the family moved into the Washington home of his maternal grandfather, Senator Gore. When his parents divorced, Vidal remained with his mother and in his early teens began calling himself Gore.

When I asked why he dropped his father's name, Vidal acknowledged nothing more complicated than practical motives. He had wanted to ease out from under the double burden of being called Eugene and Junior, neither of which he liked. Furthermore, from an early age he had harbored political aspirations and believed that the name Gore would waken in voters memories of his grandfather.

Perhaps noticing my skepticism at this explanation, Vidal stressed the seriousness of his political ambitions. At one point he had considered moving to Oklahoma and using Senator Gore's home base as his own. But when he did run for office, it was in upstate New York, in 1960, and although he lost his race for Congress, he received more votes than any Democratic candidate in that district in the last fifty years.

Bluntly I asked if he had liked his father. Just as bluntly he said he had.

Then there was another ringing interruption—the doorbell this time—and Vidal and Rat went to answer it. A delivery boy had brought a package.

I decided it was pointless to press him about his family unless I intended to indulge in a lot of loathsome penny psychology—which I didn't. I had heard rumors that Vidal had had a strained relationship with his mother, but they don't bear repeating. On balance, it seems more significant that he has spoken fondly of his father.

John Gregory Dunne, the novelist husband of Joan Didion, tells of a dinner party at which Vidal mentioned that he had just met David Eisenhower. Given his opinion of Ike —"the Great Golfer"—and Nixon, the assembled guests expected a barrage of withering criticisms. Instead, Vidal observed that he and the young Eisenhower were probably the only two men in America who had been born at West Point and had gone on to Exeter. Somehow this prompted a nostalgic reverie about Eugene Vidal, Sr.

"It was something quite rare," Dunne recalls. "You don't often hear men of Gore's age talk about their fathers the way he did that night. You could sense the genuine affection he had for the man. More than just affection. Love."

Once Vidal and Rat had settled back into the chair, we started again, stuttering along as before, interrupted every few minutes by the telephone. There were calls from friends, editors, film directors and producers. But I didn't mind. In fact, I preferred it this way, since it gave a more accurate idea of Vidal's afternoons than I would have got if he had left the phone off the hook.

More important these interruptions prevented Vidal from finding his rhythm and turning the conversation into a performance. Having watched him on television and at parties, having read many of his interviews, I knew he had a memory bank full of canned answers, quips, and well-turned epigrams. True, he delivers these lines with a panache that suggests spontaneity, but one winter in Rome as I heard him over a period of months polish a remark about Ted Kennedy—"Every declining culture deserves a King

151

Farouk"—I realized just how much work goes into his supposedly extemporaneous wit, just how much care it takes to appear insouciant.

I fed him no straight lines until I mentioned Norman Mailer and asked if he had read *The Executioner's Song*.

"No," said Vidal, his voice assuming its quotable cadences. "Life is too short and Mailer is too long." Pause. "I take that back. Mailer is short too. Isn't it ironic that our would-be most masculine writer has come to resemble—in appearance, if not art—Colette?"

The doorbell rang. The same delivery boy had come back to ask for directions to the Valley. Patiently, with no trace of the asperity of his remark about Mailer, Vidal told him which road to take.

To Vidal's detractors, few things are more offensive than his barbed comments about people. While it can be entertaining, if not always edifying, to hear him hold forth against his enemies, it is troubling to listen to him tag acquaintances with belittling nicknames and rub raw the nerves of old friends. But if on occasion he is gratuitously unkind, he more often than not hits the right mark. Personally I am inclined to forgive him his trespasses (behind my back he refers to me as Youngblood Hawke, Herman Wouk's lumbering surrogate for Thomas Wolfe) because of his talent for deflating the pompous, unmasking the fraudulent, and accusing the criminal. In this role as public scourge and defender of the rational, he is not attacking people and their personalities so much as their actions and ideas—a subtle, yet crucial, distinction.

I have the sense that Vidal is frequently accused of cruelty when, in fact, he is simply being candid, a quality not greatly appreciated in a literary community which tends to view all criticism as conspiratorial or personally motivated. Unlike so many of his fellow writers who are caught up in a frenzy of mutual backscratching—I reviewed your novel, now you blurb mine; I did an article on you, now give me an invitation to your literary conference—Vidal remains his own man and he can be austerely objective about his work, as well as that of his friends.

These same friends, however, maintain that Vidal's generosity is as dependable as his sometimes painful candor. They cite examples of money quietly lent or donated, of hospitality graciously extended, and of advice and help given to young writers. Though Vidal brushes aside questions on this subject, he has often intervened to ensure that deserving articles and novels get published. And there are any number of needy actors and actresses who continue to find roles because of his influence with filmmakers.

But laudable as his personal charity may be, Christopher Isherwood believes that Vidal's public stances are better indications of his generous spirit. "He has an admirably aggressive side," Isherwood observes, "and when he feels people's rights are being abrogated, he takes action. I remember a time in Washington when he tried to stop some policemen who were beating a black man. But he didn't let it go at that. He called the local newspaper, then did an essay on police brutality."

In Vidal's commitment to basic human rights, Isherwood feels that *The City and the Pillar* (1948) was a crucial landmark. "It was the first novel to portray homosexuality as something not sick and twisted. That was a very important step, not just for Gore, but for a great many people."

Although *The City and the Pillar* became a best-seller, Vidal paid a high price for every dollar he earned. The Good Gray Geese of American literature, as he calls them, decided the book was morally corrupt and, therefore, unacceptable. For years afterward, Vidal claims, he wasn't reviewed in some journals and could always count on shrill notices in others. As his next five novels disappeared into oblivion, his bank balance dwindled almost as rapidly as his reputation. In the late forties when he applied to the Guggenheim Foundation for a grant, he was rejected in favor of the likes of E. Howard Hunt. Yes, the same E. Howard Hunt who later proved to be as bungling a spook as he was a spy novelist.

By 1953, Vidal admits, "I was on the verge of providing future thesis writers with a poignant page or two of metropolitan suffering, before I went off to Africa to run rifles." Rather than follow in Rimbaud's footsteps, however, he supported himself by writing plays, movies, and TV scripts. It wasn't until the publication of *Julian* in 1964 that he could count on more than incidental income from his fiction.

When Vidal returned, I asked about that difficult period of his career.

"You have to keep in mind," he said, "that it wasn't just the usual fag-baiters who were after me. During the McCarthy era I was viewed as a dangerously outspoken leftist—not only a threat to the sanctity of the American family, but out to destroy the Republic. When I began spending a lot of time in Italy, that inflamed suspicions all the more. I mean, what kind of real man and real American would want to live anywhere except the home of the brave and land of the free?"

But did he really believe he got bad reviews, or none, because of his politics and his sex life?

Again he inclined his head to one side and smiled his wintry smile. "When I was nearly broke and it had become clear to me I could not get a good review anywhere, I published several mysteries under the pseudonym of Edgar Box. All of them were favorably received. But just recently when they were reissued under the name Vidal, some of the same magazines which had praised the books were now quite negative, even nasty. What would you infer?"

"You think things haven't changed then?"

"Not much."

"Ever apply for another Guggenheim?"

"Never. I've never won any literary award and today I don't believe there's one I would accept. For years I was nominated for membership in the American Academy of Arts and Letters. And every year friends who were in it told me I had been blackballed. Finally, in 1976, I was invited to become a member. But I sent a telegram: "The Academy does itself a belated honor. Unfortunately I cannot accept the invitation. I already belong to Diners Club.' "

Perhaps it is this astringency, this self-sufficiency, which has allowed Vidal to survive and has, simultaneously, invited trouble. To be accurate, he has done more than merely survive. He has flourished. Yet he gives the impression in his writing and in person of someone perpetually embattled. Perhaps he likes this position; perhaps it galvanizes him to do his best work. But it is misleading of him to imply he hasn't been well reviewed. Each of his books is emblazoned with encomiums, one of them, amazingly enough, from Norman Mailer.

Still, there is no doubt that his pronouncements about sex —especially his insistence that it is nobody's business what adults do in bed—have influenced people's opinion of him and his books. This, as Vidal has stated, is perfectly congruent with the bizarre American notion that sex is the measure of all morality and that lust in the hearts of our political officials should loom larger as a campaign issue than inflation or foreign policy.

Given the general view that Vidal is a man of questionable morals, it is ironic that his most serious failing as a novelist is his tendency to try to infuse his fiction with the same ethical concerns, the same polemical intensity, the same didactic spirit which inform his nonfiction. But while his essays manage to be stylish and urbane, as well as instructive, his weaker novels are sometimes too manipulative, too eager to make a point. Impatient with the novelist's task of moving by implication, Vidal depends too heavily on adjectives and adverbs to convey meaning that the reader would be better off discovering for himself. Instead of dramatizing scenes, as one would expect of an experienced playwright and screenwriter, he occasionally makes the elementary mistake of telling, not showing.

But at his frequent best, Vidal can smoothly integrate ideas into a story and voice his ideological concerns in the dynamic interplay of characters. He also succeeds in being most amusing when he is most serious, most imaginative when most provocative. Under different and fairer circumstances, he would be recognized as a novelist of considerable achievement and a cultural commentator of profound importance. Instead he is known best as a talk-show performer.

After yet another interruption—a typist had arrived to pick up a script—Vidal made us each a cup of strong coffee. "This stuff has killed more writers than liquor," he said. "But I can't live without it."

When I asked what he was working on now, I got a good idea why he needs coffee. A synopsis of his current projects lasted more than ten minutes.

Within the past few months he had finished a long, ambitious novel, tentatively entitled *Creation*, which took years of research and required him to master the teachings of Buddha, Confucius, and Zoroaster. Then exhausted and bored with Italy, he came to Los Angeles, feeling he needed a break from fiction writing.

So he did the filmscript for *Dress Gray*, Lucian Truscott's novel about the murder of a homosexual cadet at West Point. Then he agreed to do a screenplay about Libby Holman, who was indicted in the shooting of her tobacco-heir husband, Zachary Smith Reynolds, but was never brought to trial.

Meanwhile, in preparation for a six-hour teleplay he is scheduled to write for NBC, he has been reading all the available material on Abraham Lincoln. Now, he said, sounding slightly weary, his publishers are urging him to do a novel about Lincoln that would come out to coincide with the TV miniseries.

"Why?" I broke in. "Why keep working so hard?"

There was no pause for reflection. I had pressed a button, and out popped a line that has found its way into all his recent interviews. I had first heard it in rough draft as "The mind that doesn't feed itself eats itself." Now it had been polished into "The mind that doesn't nourish itself devours itself."

156

Not content with this canned response, I insisted there must be more to it than that.

Vidal admitted that middle age can be a time of melancholy and boredom. To hold them at bay, he kept busy.

"Would you feel guilty, would you be unhappy, if you weren't working?"

"Of course. After all," Vidal said with no trace of a smile, no echo of irony, "I'm a Puritan Moralist."

• • • • •

THE JUNK-FOOD WARS

After nine months of nonstop, no-holds-barred guerrilla warfare, the golden arches of McDonald's remain in place, and life in Rome has reached that point of uneasy, improvised truce that passes in this city for peace. True, one faction or another still fires off an occasional salvo; lawsuits are pending; a few aggrieved citizens and illegal aliens write impassioned letters to local newspapers. But the broad consensus is that the bloodiest battles are behind us and that it is best to let future generations of experts and scholars decide who was right.

Personally, I am unwilling to take the long view and wait for history's verdict. For one thing, the public record of events, even the press's description of the precise location of the combat zone, was riddled with errors. As one who saw his share of action on the front line and lived to tell the tale, I feel it is of the utmost importance to set down my impressions of the Great Hamburger War before memory fades and convictions congeal like the grease on a cold, discarded spatula.

Let me make it clear up front: I did not pick this fight. I never expected to become a partisan. Jaded and weary, perhaps even a bit cynical—picture me as Rick in *Casablanca* or a 1960s burnout case from *The Big Chill*—I intended to maintain my neutrality when the attacks and counterattacks started. I sympathized with both sides. I just didn't want to get involved.

On the one hand, like any right-thinking individual, I resented America's Coca-colonization of the world, and I experienced immense pleasure whenever people resisted a hard sell or rejected a shoddy product. (The failure of the Edsel was, for me, a rare and wondrous example of consumers exacting the ultimate revenge.) I especially decried the universal drift toward franchises, fast food, and deep-fried everything.

On the other hand, a child of my times and native land, I bought name brands, remained mindlessly loyal to many American products, and continued to consume flabbergasting quantities of dubious foodstuffs imported from the States. Peanut butter, for instance, is a staple of my diet, even though in Italy it costs not much less than caviar.

When it became clear that McDonald's, which had invaded most other European capitals, would finally license a franchise in Rome, I grumbled and clucked, publicly agreeing with those who feared that what the Carthaginians, the Visigoths, and Genghis Khan had failed to accomplish, the opening of a hamburger joint would quickly achieve. Rome would be ruined, its cultural purity sullied, its distinctive atmosphere destroyed.

Secretly, however, I knew I wouldn't join those enraged residents who called for a burger boycott, organized a mass demonstration in the Piazza di Spagna, and cooked up a most theatrical media event—a celebrity pasta eat-in on the Spanish Steps. My job as a writer, I convinced myself, was to observe, not act; to report, not participate. When the first wave of highly vocal conflict died down, I set out for McDonald's with the dual excuse that I was doing research and at the same time giving my sons a greasy taste of their homeland.

On a day that would prove to be full of sharp reversals of expectation, the first surprise was that we had trouble finding the place. Though all the news and TV stories, both in Italy and in America, had emphasized that McDonald's had set up shop in the Piazza de Spagna—one got the impression that the golden arches loomed in gruesome neon over the Spanish Steps—it is actually located a long city block away from the bottom of the steps, on Via Due Macelli. Instead of the usual blinding parabolas, this McDonald's has a modest sign in brown and white that cannot be seen from any of the famous monuments that it has been accused of desecrating. What's more, although Valentino filed suit saying that his nearby couturier studio was being overwhelmed by the stench of fried food, the area smells, just as it always has, of exhaust fumes from cars and manure from horses drawing carriages.

Inside the restaurant, there were other surprises. The place was packed—with Italians, not Americans—and unlike the archetypal fast-food shack, aglitter with glass, Formica, and plastic, this Roman McDonald's is an upscale operation. Supposedly the largest McDonald's franchise in the world, it has seating for several hundred, and it is decorated with glazed-tile mosaics, marble floors, a waterfall, antique amphorae, and murals of the city as viewed from various hills. In addition to the standard fare, there's a wide selection of salads, including *caprese,* a tasty combination of tomato and mozzarella slices seasoned with basil and olive oil.

My boys and I stuck to the basics—burgers, fries, and shakes. But we decided to eat outdoors, partly because we wanted to sit in the sun, partly because I wanted to put some journalistic distance between McDonald's and me and mull over what I had seen so far. We strolled to the Spanish Steps, found a few square feet of empty space, and settled down to have lunch. Surrounded by guitar strummers and student backpackers of all creeds and colors, accosted by street urchins, winos, artists with sketch pads, and hustlers selling fake Gucci bags and Rolex wristwatches, I felt we were supremely inconspicuous, and I was free to continue my research by asking my kids for their opinion of the food.

We hadn't been there two minutes when an American woman in clunky jogging shoes heard us speaking English and descended upon us. Since she was carrying a Michelin guide, I thought she wanted to ask directions. Quite to the contrary, she meant to give them.

"You should be ashamed of yourself," she said in a piercing voice. "Don't pretend you don't understand me." Of all the lowlifes and lollygaggers on the steps, she had somehow singled me out for her opprobrium.

"What did I do?" I asked, echoing the whiny, adenoidal question often posed by my boys.

"You know what I'm talking about. Why travel all the way to Italy and then feed your children that trash? It's bad enough that you eat it at home."

After an instant of tongue-tied confusion, I lamely answered, "We didn't travel here. We live here."

"That's even worse."

"We never eat it at home."

"You shouldn't eat it at all. Buy these boys a decent Italian meal." With that, she stalked away.

"Who's she?" my six-year-old asked. "Your teacher?"

"Dad doesn't have a teacher," my irate eleven-year-old objected. "Why didn't you talk back to her? Why didn't you tell her off?"

"Let's just finish our lunch," I answered. But I dropped my own half-eaten burger into its Styrofoam box and sat there stewing. Why *hadn't* I talked back? Why did we Americans overseas always swallow so much guff—and not only from the locals but also from other Americans? Although I was too furious to eat it now, what was so bad about American fast food? Italians had pizza by the oil-laden slab and those deep-fried rice balls they call *suppli*. Greeks had

161

gyros. The English gobbled fish and chips. The French had —why, it dawned on me with all the force of a major discovery—they had french fries! They invented them! And no one made fun of their cuisine.

Suddenly, sitting there on one of the world's best-known staircases, I was struck by what the French refer to as *l'esprit de l'escalier,* the wit of the staircase—those clever comebacks you think of as you're leaving the scene of an embarrassing incident. In a great rush, I realized all the things I might have—no, should have!—said in answer to the graceless lady in jogging shoes. I made up my mind that there would be no more neo-isolationism for me, no more fence-straddling in the food wars. I had found out whose side I was on, and I was fully prepared to point out the errors of the opposition.

What sense did it make for Italians to assert their cultural purity by eating pasta? After all, pasta was a Chinese dish brought back by Marco Polo.

And why pick on McDonald's when there has for decades been fast food of all kinds in Italy? Outside almost every historic site in Rome there stands a trailer advertising hot dogs, potato chips, Cokes, doughnuts, and sandwiches. In fact, I abruptly realized, there was one parked right at the top of the Spanish Steps. Had the self-righteous lady gone up to read them the riot act?

And what about all the other hamburger dives in Rome? To my knowledge, nobody had ever complained—certainly there had never been mass demonstrations—about the Wimpy Bar on Via Veneto or the Big Burg in the Piazza Barberini or the Cowboy just off swank Via Sistina; about Arnold's across the street from the Piazza Navona or Bar Viola around the corner from the Pantheon. And talk about desecration, talk about sacrilege! Standing no farther from St. Peter's Square than McDonald's does from the Spanish Steps there's Ma Burger, with its huge illuminated sign showing sizzling meat patties shooting out of the muzzle of an M-16 rifle.

While my boys went on munching their burgers, I was really warming to the subject, spotting ironies left and right, imagining witty, withering responses I'd fling in her face if that arrogant bat ever crossed my path again, if anyone ever hassled me for the mere fact that I was eating fast food from my own country. I mean, in New York City, did I bug Italians about all the pizzerias along Second Avenue? So give me and other Americans a break already. That's all McDonald's is saying, isn't it? We deserve a break.

"Look at that," I cried out to my sons. I pointed toward the bottom of the steps, at Babington's Tea Room. "Nobody raises a fuss about it. And what does it sell? Treacle and custard that'd rot your teeth."

They nodded sagely.

"What do we have to be ashamed of?" I asked my boys, who were eating happily but starting to eye me strangely.

"Nothing," they shouted. "You should have told her off."

"Next time I will."

Ever since then, I've been waiting for my chance and polishing my put-downs. Once a week, my sons and I go to McDonald's, order take-out food, and sit in some public place, regular Rambos with chips on our shoulders, prickly with burger pride, just begging somebody to make our day. I know price comparisons, nutritional values, and cholesterol counts. I've done my homework, and I'm prepared to counter whatever the enemy shoots in my direction.

But for the moment, at least, the truce is holding. As a matter of fact, Italians seem to be assimilating the fast-food invasion as smoothly as they have swallowed up every other foreign intrusion. For centuries, you see, they have had plenty of practice at disarming enemies, subtly conquering them even as they appear to be capitulating, gradually changing outsiders who think they are imposing their will. Within a year or two, look for McDonald's to test-market cheeseburgers with marinara sauce somewhere in America.

♦ ♦ ♦ ♦ ♦

MONTE CARLO

For decades tennis has served as a cornerstone of the spring social season in Monte Carlo, and with the finals scheduled for Easter Sunday, the tournament has always started on the preceding Monday. At least as far as the public was concerned, it started Monday. Although there were always qualifying rounds, these prompted little or no interest. But this year was different. This year Bjorn Borg was making a comeback, and because he had refused to play ten Grand Prix events, he had to qualify.

Borg had to qualify! To many people in and out of tennis, the idea sounded absurd. After a five-month layoff he was still ranked number 4 in the world. To force him to qualify . . . why, it was like making Muhammad Ali fight in the Golden Gloves, like putting Pélé back on a vacant lot in Brazil with a ball fashioned out of old rags, like shunting Niki Lauda into the slow lane, like expecting Joe Namath to employ a dating service.

It was all the fault of tennis politics, newspapers complained, all part of the war between WCT and the Grand

Prix. If you were a member of the Pro Council, you could attempt to explain that the ten-tournament rule was reasonable, that without it the top players would concentrate on exhibitions and let the tournament system that supported the rest of the players wither and die. You could, like Sandy Mayer, point out "the greed" in Borg's schedule. You could accuse the Swede of limiting himself to "shopping expeditions" at Grand Slam events. But, finally, you were wasting your breath. For most people, Bjorn Borg was a great champion and a fine gentleman, and it was ridiculous to force him to qualify.

Ridiculous it may have been, but it was also a box-office bonanza. The tournament in Monte Carlo was quick to realize this, and it announced that the event would officially begin on April 1. The qualies attracted two hundred journalists and several dozen photographers. General admission was $5 for the first three days and $10 for the finals on Sunday—the finals of the qualies, that is.

That week several mass-circulation magazines carried features on Bjorn and Mariana Borg. *Paris Match* ran a cover photo of the young couple embracing, and a cloying article praised their love match. The Borgs were said to be planning a family—presumably long-range planning, since Mariana and Borg hadn't been living together lately. Still, Mariana held out the fervent hope that children would arrive within a few years.

My own family had arrived more promptly from Rome. A friend had lent us his apartment outside of Cannes, and I became a commuter. Each morning my wife drove me down to the tiny station in La Bocca, where I boarded a train for Monte Carlo, thirty miles up the coast. On one side of the track the Mediterranean spread like a cerulean platter toward a horizon lost in haze. On the other side the purple hills of Provence, flecked with yellow mimosa and dark-green cypresses, rose toward the Maritime Alps, whose peaks were still snow-capped.

Most of the passengers appeared to be tourists and day-trippers. But there was also a colorful contingent of blacks who hustled fake ivory carvings, glass beads, fly whisks, snakeskin wallets, and leather bush hats. I imagined a vast factory in Marseilles mass-producing African kitsch and sending out these poor souls to sell it. I never saw anybody buy a thing.

The train passed through Cannes, curved along the beach at Golfe Juan, cut through Juan les Pins and came to Antibes. Then it was on to Nice and the breath-catching bay at Villefranche and the tiny town of Beaulieu, which, viewed through a fringe of palm fronds, lived up to its name, Beautiful Place. And finally, just before Monaco, there was the modest village of Cap d'Ail, the garlic cape, home of those humble workers who swept the streets, serviced the condos, and drove the limos of the tax-free enclave next door.

It should have been a pleasant trip. But I had just had an umpire tell me enough about professional tennis to fill me with despair. I wasn't on my way to the Monte Carlo Country Club to watch Bjorn Borg make his comeback. I was on my way there to try to find out whether he had rigged a match with John McEnroe.

Like everybody on the circuit that winter, I had talked and thought incessantly about Bjorn Borg. Despite all that had been said and written about him, I decided that nobody had taken a comprehensive look at the man and attempted to piece together the incongruent shards of his character. This, of course, presumed that he had a character, that he wasn't simply a billboard, a blank page on which advertisers could scrawl their messages.

Borg seemed to me to have struck a Faustian bargain at some point in his young life and agreed to transform himself into an automaton in return for being made into the best tennis player in the world. Now a model of lobotomized decorum on court and off, he was praised as much for his tunnel vision and his remorseless one-dimensionality as for his metronomical ground strokes. With the tacit approval of the public and the cooperation of the press, he had suppressed every other aspect of his personality and ordered his existence to a single limited purpose. Each known fact about his life reinforced the notion that he was a sort of extraterrestrial being, alien yet friendly, and a fine example for kids.

He was said to have a pulse rate of thirty-five beats a minute, half that of the average human. He was said to sleep twelve hours a day. He was said to read Donald Duck comics and watch television during his spare time. A high-school dropout at the age of fourteen, he was said to be quite bright. A multimillionaire, he was said to have sound basic values. A tax exile in Monte Carlo, he was said to be a homebody.

Regardless of what he later became—in image, if not in reality—he didn't start off as a poker-faced, exemplary little boy. According to Peter Bodo's *Inside Tennis,* he "was an only child, and Saturday was designated as his day with his father, Rune. All Bog wanted to do was play competitive games . . . but when he lost, he would cry and carry on until he was sent up to bed. Many Saturdays ended in an early appointment with the sandman, until little Bjorn calmed down a bit and learned to suppress his frustration. Inside, he remained furious."

As an adolescent he was still volatile, a screamer of obscenities, an enraged racket-thrower. When the Swedish tennis federation suspended him for six months, his conduct improved, but even after he set out on the international tour, he could be foul-tempered, headstrong, and obstreperous. During a practice session he and his coach, Lennart Bergelin, once got into a shouting match and nearly came to blows. When Bergelin smacked him on the head with a box of balls, Borg called his parents and threatened to quit tennis.

Although he never gave up the game altogether, he got a reputation for giving up in important matches. When the calls or the crowd were against him, he sometimes stalked off court and refused to return. Other times, when an opponent got the best of him, he stayed on court, but acted as if he didn't care whether he won or lost, and whenever questioned about his moody, unprofessional behavior, he refused to speak to reporters.

During this early period there was another spicy component to his image. With his long blond locks and lean Nordic face, he was portrayed as a heartbreaker pursued everywhere by groupies. One British newspaper went so far as to print a photograph—a palpable fake—of Borg unbuckling his belt for a tryst in Hyde Park.

Then, miraculously, within the space of a year or two, all this was forgotten and Borg underwent a sea change so dramatic that nobody dared remind people of his previous incarnation. By the time he won his first Wimbledon title at the age of twenty, he had shucked his reputation as a quitter and a playboy and acquired the image that has stayed with him—unflappable, indefatigable, impervious to pressure, impassive in victory or defeat, the Ice Man, the perfect machine.

Not until the emergence of John McEnroe did Borg begin to reveal his first serious cracks and fissures. To be beaten by a player whose moods were so transparent, whose emotions spilled forth like a spendthrift's money, and whose demeanor was so offensive must have been truly shattering to the Swede. How else explain his behavior during his last full year of competition?

In a match against McEnroe at the 1981 Volvo Masters, he objected to a call and refused to play on. Confronting the umpire, Mike Lugg, he kept mumbling, "Ask the linesman, ask the linesman." He spoke as if in a trance and never once during the incident blinked his eyes, not even when he was given a warning, then a point penalty. Desperate not to default him, Mike Lugg had to summon the Supervisor to convince Borg to continue the match.

Then at the 1981 U.S. Open, having already lost his Wimbledon crown and having just been crushed by McEnroe, he regressed to childhood. Live, on international television, he walked off before the prize-giving ceremony. Newsmen and TV commentators, anxious to preserve the image they had helped create, claimed Borg wasn't a poor sport. Due to a death threat, they said, Borg had been placed under police protection and whisked away from Louis Armstrong Stadium.

In fact, there *had* been a death threat. But Borg knew nothing about it when he left McEnroe, the tournament promoters, and television announcers stranded at the net. "I was just very, very disappointed," he later admitted. "I couldn't face the idea of making a nice speech in front of all those people. I suppose I was a bad boy."

It struck me as the first entirely spontaneous thing Borg had done in years. Trapped for so long like a carcass in ice, he had warmed to his own emotions and awakened.

As the train rocked along the tracks to Monte Carlo, it intrigued me to consider the possibility that the robot had rebelled, the computer had willfully shut down, the automaton had determined to reclaim its humanity. Was there in Borg's long layoff and in his reluctance to commit himself again full-time to the tour a parable of redemption?

◆ ◆ ◆ ◆ ◆

The Monte Carlo Country Club, site of the tournament, isn't in Monte Carlo. It clings to a craggy cliff just over the border in France. When I asked whether the tax-free privilege extended to the club, I was answered with the same stares of mute disbelief which met any question about homosexuality on the men's tour. In Monaco, money may be an all-pervasive obsession, but it is a passion that dares not speak its name—at least not to the press.

A series of terraces, like steps designed for a giant, descend from the Moyenne Corniche to the sea, with practice courts on top, then the sprawling clubhouse, then a patio with chairs and tables, then the show court, then a parking lot. The clay courts, the tablecloths, and the clubhouse are all much the same salmon-pink color. Beyond a stand of cypresses that serve as a windscreen at the far end of the show court, the blue of the Mediterranean meets the paler blue of the sky.

The press box, situated just below the lunch tables on the patio, offers an excellent view of everything except tennis. Gazing down at the court through a grillwork of green railings, I could, if I sat up straight, see both players, but not the net. If I slumped in my seat, I could see the net, but not the near baseline.

Set off at a discreet distance from the court, photographers knelt on a carpet, keeping a vigil for Borg. They hadn't been there for the previous match and they wouldn't wait around for the next. Similarly, most spectators—and there were more than a thousand, a decent crowd at any tournament—wouldn't stay to watch the other qualifiers.

The ball boys and linesmen marched to their posts wearing beautiful powder-blue outfits provided by Ellesse. The promotional strips around the court showed a bias toward high fashion—Céline, Piaget, Jacomo, and Benetton. Yet Borg came on looking like the kind of character Monte Carlo's omnipresent police would regard with rabid suspicion. Unshaven, his long hair lank and dirty, he wore a rumpled gray velour Fila warm-up.

Generally, the principality has no patience with the young, the long-haired, and the unwashed. The *New York Times* once called the place a "capitalist pustule" and said it had "a Mississippi-in-the-mid-fifties mentality." But under the correct circumstances it can be as up-to-date as a newly minted dollar. It welcomed Borg, as well as Vilas, Clerc, and several lower-ranked players, just as it had welcomed a host of Grand Prix race-car drivers. It didn't much care whether these men actually lived here. Why shouldn't Borg, a tax exile from Sweden, become a residential exile from Monte Carlo and buy a villa on Cap Ferrat in France? Prince Rainier remained more than willing to provide a refuge from various revenue agents so long as the tennis players participated in the annual tournament and the racers entered the Grand Prix every May.

While Borg was stony-faced and serious, his opponent, Paolo Bertolucci, Italy's "Pasta Kid," was utterly relaxed. The ATP Media Guide listed Bertolucci at 170 pounds, which is probably a twenty-pound underestimate. But why quibble? Paolo soon figured to be fatter.

"Thanks to Borg, I'll stuff myself," he told reporters. "I had a bet with some friends that I'd wind up playing Borg in the qualifying. Each one owes me ten dinners.

"It's a strange business," Bertolucci said. "I've had some good results in my career. I've won tournaments in Hamburg, Florence, Berlin, and Barcelona. But now that I'm twenty-eight and playing the qualies, I'm a star overnight. I've never given so many interviews, I've never been followed by photographers before today. I've never taken a set from Borg, but I'm happy to play him. At least I won't lose to some unknown guy."

Lose he did. Bertolucci held a service break and seemed in control of the first set, but Borg managed to pull even, then broke to win 7–5. The second set was a formality, 6–0.

The consensus was that Borg looked rusty, indecisive, and vulnerable. At a press conference Bertolucci confirmed that anybody in the top thirty could have beaten Borg today. Although the Swede didn't respond to that, he admitted there had been moments when he felt "deconcentrated." For the next week he would make himself sound like frozen orange juice—concentrated one minute, deconcentrated the next.

When a journalist suggested that, much as he might not like playing the qualies, he needed them to regain his timing and match-toughness, Borg didn't see it that way. It was stupid, he said, to force him to qualify. The Pro Council had made a mistake with its ten-tournament rule and he demanded they change it. Unless they did, he might not defend his French Open title. He might skip Wimbledon as well. These weren't idle threats, he declared. He had no intention of compromising. The Pro Council had made the mistake, not he, and he wasn't going to help them save face.

Borg left the room before I could reach him. When I tried to arrange an interview through one of the tournament press officers, he gave me the same glazed look I had got when I inquired about the Country Club's tax status. Everyone wanted to speak personally to Bjorn, the press officer said, and he didn't want to talk to anybody, not even to *Sports Illustrated* or the London *Sunday Times*. I'd just have to ask my questions at the daily press conference.

I explained that mine weren't the kinds of questions that could be asked in public. To which the man replied, those were precisely the kinds of questions Borg detested. I could write him a letter or try to pass a message through his coach, Lennart Bergelin, or his agents at IMG. But, frankly, the press officer thought I was wasting my time.

◆ ◆ ◆ ◆ ◆

Over the weekend and on Monday, while Bjorn Borg reduced two more qualifiers to smoky rubble, then started play in the main draw, I continued my attempts to reach him, and as I did so, I became better acquainted with Monte Carlo and its Country Club. I even bumped into the Grimaldis—quite literally bumped into them at the buffet lunch, which journalists got to eat for a mere $15 while the public had to pay $22. Princess Grace wore large sunglasses and a floppy straw hat that hid her pale, plump face. With her were Princess Stephanie, looking like a street gamine in tight jeans, a T-shirt, and gobs of makeup, and Prince Albert, also in jeans and T-shirt, but looking like a young banker who had gone slumming.

Perhaps I should have asked Prince Albert to help me reach Borg. With his Walkman headset, its antenna quivering, the Prince appeared to be maintaining communications with sources throughout the hemisphere. Surely he could contact the reclusive Swede.

As I watched several early-round matches, I wondered

whether any other sport was played under such drastically varied conditions. This past Sunday, Ivan Lendl and Peter McNamara had met in the finals of a tournament on a fast indoor carpet under artificial lights in Frankfurt. Now, two days later, they were outdoors on clay, contending with the sun and wind of the Côte d'Azur and having trouble with lowly opponents.

Indoors, outdoors, daytime, nighttime, carpeted courts, cement courts, composition courts, European clay, American clay, English grass, Australian grass—each new condition demanded an adjustment from a player. Blessed with more raw talent than McNamara, Lendl had less trouble regearing his game. After saving one set point, he rolled past a Chilean, Pedro Rebolledo, 7–5/6–2. But McNamara never found his rhythm and fell to the pint-size German Peter Elter, 6–3/6–2.

There were also serious psychological adjustments exacted by professional tennis. For Chris Lewis, a gifted player from New Zealand, the price of coming so far in his career has been constant fear and he has never shown any reluctance to admit it. Lewis is terrified of flying. Yet if he wants to go on playing, he knows he has to spend hundreds of hours in airplanes, and still more hours on the ground dreading the next flight. With a pharmacopoeia of tranquilizers—Mogadon, Tranxine, Equanil, Valium—he copes as best he can and arranges his schedule to restrict his time in the air. He also keeps cars on three continents—Australia, Europe, and America—and drives to tournaments whenever possible.

Still, for all his planning, there are frequent complications. He had just flown from Australia to Germany, where he was supposed to pick up a new Mercedes and motor down to Monte Carlo. But when the Mercedes wasn't ready, he had had to rent a car and hadn't arrived here until Sunday night. The thirty-hour flight from Australia, then the long drive from Frankfurt, plus the fact that "I was loaded up with pills," resulted in the inevitable. Facing Guillermo Vilas in the first round, he played like "a piece of garbage" and lost 6–1/6–1.

♦ ♦ ♦ ♦ ♦

Next day I came close to Bjorn Borg, but there was no chance to talk to him. He swept into the press lounge for what politicians call "a photo opportunity." Nicola Pietrangeli and Ilie Nastase were with him. Pietrangeli stroked Nastase's Adidas sweater. "That's nice," he said. "Do they make them for men, too?"

Nastase and Borg, the journalists, assorted sycophants, and hangers-on guffawed. Only Bambino, Nastase's bodyguard, was unamused. Or rather, he was amusing himself in a different manner. He had cornered one of the hostesses, pressing his Falstaffian belly against her slender frame. "I kiss all the pretty girls."

When the photographers had finished, people swarmed over Borg and indulged in a feverish laying on of hands. Pietrangeli hugged him, Nastase squeezed his shoulder. Reporters patted him on the back. Tournament officials caressed him. Women kissed him. Finally, Bambino hugged and kissed him, too.

Far from icy or aloof, Borg appeared giddy with pleasure. He giggled and kept mumbling in answer to all questions, "Beautiful. Everything is beautiful. Just beautiful."

Before they left, I asked Bambino whether it was true, as I had read in a newspaper, that Nastase had given him a $9,000 ring he had won in a raffle.

Bambino laughed and replied with his version of "no comment": "Journalists are shit."

♦ ♦ ♦ ♦ ♦

The following day, in a fashion familiar to commuters the world over, things fell apart. I arrived at the station to discover that the 10:24 train had been canceled. Since the next train wasn't due until 11:23, I bought a newspaper and read it over a second cup of coffee that set my pulse racing and my mind jumping about. The 11:23 turned out to be two filthy cars, already crowded to overflowing. I stood up as far as Antibes, where most passengers got off and I sat down. The relief was short-lived, however. A conductor announced there was trouble on the tracks ahead and everybody had to switch to a bus to Nice.

A minor inconvenience, I decided. I might be a few minutes late for the start of the Bjorn Borg–Adriano Panatta match. But there were worse things than riding in a clean, comfortable bus along the Mediterranean coast. The next train to Monte Carlo was scheduled to leave Nice at noon and I assumed we would arrive in time to catch it. Even if we were a few minutes late, I assumed it would wait for connecting passengers.

I assumed wrong on both counts. We reached the station just as the train was pulling out; the next one wasn't due for an hour. Since I had already wasted almost two hours covering twenty miles, the idea of another delay was insupportable.

"Why didn't the train wait for us?" I asked a lady at the information desk.

"I don't know."

"Who does know?"

"I don't know."

"Who should know?"

"I don't know."

"This is the information bureau, isn't it?"

She shrugged, bored by my questions.

"I'd like to speak to the person in charge here," I said.

She waved vaguely. "He's gone."

"When will he be back?"

"I don't know." The woman must have employed Ivan Lendl as a dialogue coach.

"Who does know?"

"I don't know."

"What's your name?" I asked, lowering my voice malevolently like a man who might have some influence with the Railroad Commissioner.

She remained unimpressed. "I don't have to tell you that."

"Why? Don't you know your name?"

"I don't have to tell you anything," she snapped.

"You *haven't* told me anything." My voice rose and ignominiously cracked.

"I told you the hour of the next train. It comes at one o'clock. Pleasant journey, monsieur."

I barged out of the station and, with an hour to kill, went to eat lunch. Next door was a fast-food outlet called Flunch. Flunch for lunch! I should have known better. But it looked harmless enough—looked, in fact, like a simulacrum of McDonald's, right down to the menu, which offered *frites,* milk shakes, and a choice of Burger Simple, Burger Fromage, or Burger Big.

"Big Burger, *s'il vous plaît,* " I said to the girl at the counter.

"You want what?"

"Big Burger," I repeated.

"Ça n'existe pas, " she said. "That doesn't exist." Not that they were out of it or no longer sold it. No, it simply didn't exist.

I pointed to the menu.

"Alors, " she said, smiling. "You mean *Burger Big.* I didn't understand. You see, in French the adjective comes after the noun. You should learn our language."

"It's *my* language!" I bellowed. " 'Burger' and 'big' are English."

"As you wish," she muttered.

"That's what I wish. A Big Burger!"

But I was lying. What I wished was to lay waste all of

France. Where else in the world would one have to endure a lecture on grammar from a fast-food cashier?

♦ ♦ ♦ ♦ ♦

Of course the one-o'clock train was late. Of course I arrived at the Country Club quivering with rage, nervous exhaustion, and nausea—the Burger Big had lodged somewhere in my esophagus. But I figured the worst had to be behind me as I settled down to watch the rest of the Borg–Adriano Panatta match, which was knotted at a set apiece and three games all in the third set.

Other members of the press were in no better mood than I. The day was overcast and chilly, yet they had come dressed to work on their tans. Fortunately, I had had the foresight to wear a ski parka.

Borg got a service break, thanks to a double fault by Adriano Panatta. But then, unlike the old Borg, who seldom slipped when he was in the lead, he had difficulty clinging to his advantage. Serving sloppily, he gave Panatta several chances to break back, and if the Italian wasn't equal to the opportunity, that had less to do with the Swede's iron will than with Panatta's poor play.

At the press conference, reporters were interested in Panatta only to the extent that he could comment on Borg's shaky form. Once they had Borg in front of them, they abruptly shifted gears and were less interested in his form than in whether he would play Wimbledon. For British journalists, this was a favorite subject, their singular obsession.

Although I believed a public press conference was the wrong place to ask whether Borg had rigged a match with McEnroe, there seemed other questions that should have intrigued journalists more than the odds on his playing Wimbledon. Repeatedly he had recited the short list of Grand Prix tournaments he had deigned to enter in 1982.

But I wanted to know how many exhibition matches he would play this year.

As the room turned ominously silent, he fixed upon me what Russell Davies of the London *Sunday Times* has referred to as "those mutely piercing narrow eyes . . . I'm sure the Turin Shroud is one of his old towels." After a significant pause Borg said, "I have no idea. I play the Suntory Cup in Tokyo. After that, I don't know."

"Let's forget the rest of the year. What's your exhibition schedule for the next three months?"

"I—have—no—idea." The words, spaced for emphasis, fell on that cowed roomful of journalists like icy slabs from a glacier.

"The next month, then?" I persisted.

"I—have—no—idea."

As every reporter knew, but few had informed their readers, Borg's tournament schedule consisted exclusively of events where he had endorsement contracts or where his agents at IMG served as promoters. Whether these constituted illegal inducements or not, they obviously provided an added incentive. I assumed, as did most people in tennis, that that was why Borg was willing to qualify for those seven tournaments, but refused to do so at Roland Garros and Wimbledon, where he had no incentive except the same prize money available to everyone else.

Yet when I asked Borg why he played the qualies here and would again in Las Vegas, but not at the Grand Slam events, he muttered that he had to put his foot down somewhere.

Why didn't he put it down in Monte Carlo?

"I decided to give the Pro Council until the French Open to change the rule."

I waited for other journalists to follow up on my questions. I had broken the ice. All they had to do was dive into the cold water with me. But they were less interested in whether his tax deal locked him into the Monte Carlo tournament than in the shakiness of his first serve.

Borg returned to his orange-juice metaphor. He said he was still feeling deconcentrated.

◆ ◆ ◆ ◆ ◆

As at most Grand Prix events, there was a tournament for the press in Monte Carlo and I had entered, thinking it would be a welcome diversion. Now I wasn't so sure. I had yet to recover from the nerve-racking train ride and the nauseating lunch, and my encounter with Borg had done nothing to improve my digestion. Still, I decided to go ahead with my match.

Upstairs in the clubhouse, in a room reserved for umpires, ball boys, and journalists, I put on my tennis shorts and shoes. It was an elegant, old-fashioned changing room with oak-paneled walls, wooden benches, and lockers. Since all the lockers were filled, I hung my clothes on a hook, as I had seen others do.

Then I wondered what to do with my watch and wallet. Surely they would be safe here. After all, this was Monte Carlo, cops were ubiquitous, crime was said to be nonexistent, and several officious attendants oversaw the changing room. But finally I dropped my valuables into a racket cover and carried them onto the court.

Two hours later, having been run ragged by a diminutive Japanese photographer, I returned to the changing room and found my clothes in a damp knot on the floor. My pants pockets had been ripped inside out. My ski parka and equipment bag were gone.

Calling one of the attendants, I pointed to the pile of clothes. "I've been robbed."

He was irate—at me, not the thief. "It's not my fault."

"I didn't say it was. But I thought you'd like to know there are robbers in your locker room."

"I'm not responsible. I can't watch everything."

I lacked the energy to argue. After showering and pulling on my disheveled clothes, I went outside, pondering the revelation that crime wasn't nonexistent in Monte Carlo, just ignored. I stopped by the press room to pick up the transcript of Borg's press conference. Generally, such transcripts give the essence, if not the entirety, of each question and answer. But the transcript of Borg's interview contained neither my questions nor his evasive responses.

◆ ◆ ◆ ◆ ◆

Despite Borg's erratic performance thus far, few would have predicted what transpired in the quarterfinals. It wasn't that the Swede played badly. He barely played at all and appeared not to care how lackadaisical he looked. Once a paragon of patience, he now rushed the net behind punchless approach shots. When serving, he usually stuffed the spare ball into his pocket, but today he kept it in his left hand, which made it impossible for him to hit his two-fisted backhand. Yannick Noah had little trouble breaking Borg twice and holding his own serve three times at love.

Yet, even after Borg dropped the first set 6–1, the crowd expected him to rally. They had seen him come back before; they were convinced he could do it again today. So it was doubly upsetting to watch him shamble through the second set, detached and absent-minded. Once he lost track of the score and started to serve from the wrong side. Another time he hit a short lob and, not bothering to wait for Noah to smash it away, he strolled to his chair and sat down. By the end of the match, if he was anxious about anything, it was only to get off the court.

At the press conference Noah sounded as incredulous as the crowd had been. "I could hear him whistling to himself during change-overs. I didn't know what to think. Was he trying to win?"

In Noah's opinion, Borg stood no chance of regaining his championship form unless he played more. "Maybe if he plays a lot of exhibitions, that might help, but not as much as tournaments would."

Bjorn Borg arrived looking as impassive and uncaring as he had on court. Witnesses in the locker room claimed that he had shuffled in whistling and dumped his rackets on the floor. Yet he told reporters he didn't remember whistling during the match. He couldn't account for what Noah heard and he didn't want to discuss it.

No, he wasn't disappointed. How could he be disappointed, he asked, when "I felt all the time I was outside the match? And when you're not in a match, you try to do something different. You rush, but you don't realize you rush. I must be more patient."

Still, he said, he was satisfied to reach the quarterfinals after such a long layoff. Perhaps it was to demonstrate his satisfaction that he left the press conference whistling.

♦ ♦ ♦ ♦ ♦

In the past it was rare for Borg to celebrate publicly even after a triumph. So it was nothing short of astounding when he showed up at Jimmy'Z after his calamitous loss to Noah.

In the purple, throbbing prose of *Society*, a flak magazine published by the Société des Bains de Mer, Jimmy'Z is a discothèque "presided over by the 'Queen of the Night' ... Régine herself." It's a place "where crazy celebrities can dance until dawn just like the princesses in the fairy tale. ... Jimmy'Z is young and fearless, and open to the stars, and all are free to laugh and dance and mix with the rich, the beautiful, and the bizarre, who may be loaded down with precious jewels or covered in magnificent evening gowns; it doesn't matter, the moonlight performs a strange magic and all the world is young again and we are suddenly and quite inexplicably bewitched."

Without a doubt, Borg acted bewitched, whether by the disco beat or some basic change in body chemistry, it would be impossible to say. While José Luis Clerc chatted up Princess Stephanie—the Princess appeared to have a crush on Argentinians; earlier in the week she had been observed

doing cartwheels beside Vilas' practice court—Borg preferred to dance with Nastase's bodyguard, Bambino, who had
appropriated a tablecloth and bath towel to dress himself in
drag.

The next evening Borg skipped a scheduled appearance
at a cocktail party where he was to receive a special award
for excellence. He left Monte Carlo and was rumored to have
gone to Geneva or Tokyo or Cairo. Wherever he went, he
was unreachable. When I called his agents at the International Management Group, I was shunted from person to
person until a perky woman with a British accent asked what
she could do for me. I said that I had been told by an umpire
that he had overheard Bjorn Borg and John McEnroe arranging to split the first two sets of a match to make it more
exciting and to fill a television time-slot. Would Borg or the
IMG agency care to comment? Still perky, still upbeat and
positive, the lady said there would be no comment.

Soon afterward, Borg announced that he wouldn't play
the French Open or Wimbledon. He was canceling his entire
schedule of tournament events and would henceforth participate in nothing but exhibitions. In effect, he had become the
first of a new breed. Just as players during the shamateur
era routinely turned professional as soon as they won a
major title that would get them a good contract, Borg had
quit the pro tour as soon as it no longer served his purposes.
For years competitive tournament tennis had been a minor
part of his program, just a form of advertising that kept his
price at astronomical levels for commercial endorsements
and exhibitions. Now at the age of twenty-six he had decided
to devote himself full time to the most lucrative divisions of
the sport/business—marketing and entertainment.

John McEnroe wasn't any easier to reach than Borg, but
his father, John Sr., who served as his lawyer and agent,
granted an interview and although he complained that he
didn't have much time to talk to me, he rambled on and on
until the cassette on my tape recorder ran out an hour later.

Mr. McEnroe Sr. seemed to have the metabolism of a jockey. As he spoke, he jawed on a stick of chewing gum; he fiddled with a pair of nail clippers; he put his feet up on his desk; he scratched his face; he gestured histrionically with his hands, his left gleaming with a fat gold watch and a ring as big as a walnut; he tugged at his knee-length socks. He was lively as a leprechaun—a hard-bitten leprechaun with a New York accent full of grit and vinegar instead of blarney.

When I told him about the match that his son and Borg were alleged to have rigged, he began to stammer and labor for *le mot juste.* "I know of no such, uh, I'm not saying, as I said before, it never happened. I know of no such . . ." He groped for words to describe what he hadn't known. Leaning back in the chair, he slipped a hand under the waistband of his trousers, reached down and rearranged his private parts. Perhaps he had learned this move from Jimmy Connors. "I'd be inclined to think that's probably not too likely in John's case. But, uh, I'm not trying, again, I'm not trying, I'm not commenting on that with respect to John. I just don't, I don't know that that's so. I would doubt it. Although I don't want to sound naive, I realize that there are times when that may make a certain amount of sense."

"Why?" I asked.

"If they were doing it from an entertainment-value viewpoint, that may make sense at times. I mean, if it's something that's labeled an exhibition and is nothing more than an exhibition. Uh, that may be, uh, not terrible."

In fact, it wasn't labeled as an exhibition, but Mr. McEnroe Sr. rushed on with his disclaimer. "As I said, I do not know of it and, uh, in any of the events with which I am associated, which are very few—which are none." He burst out laughing. "I'm not associated with any of them." Yet with respect to all those events with which he was not associated, he asserted, "It doesn't go on. It wouldn't go on."

"Would that trouble you legally?" I asked. "I mean, if these matches were broadcast, for example, or televised and something like that was going on?"

Mr. McEnroe's volubility evaporated and he subsided into silence for several moments. Then he said, "I've never given it a moment's thought, to be perfectly honest with you. I've never given it a moment's thought."

◆ ◆ ◆ ◆ ◆

HOT TICKETS

In a city of three million people, with a large diplomatic corps, a sizable expatriate community, and tens of thousands of English-speaking tourists passing through every week, you'd think it would be easy to see an American or British film in its original language. But you'd be wrong. You are more likely to find a subtitled Italian movie at your neighborhood theater in the United States.

Make no mistake. American films are popular in Rome, drawing large enthusiastic crowds, prompting long erudite reviews in daily newspapers, and resulting in incessant interviews with the stars on TV and in slick magazines. *Top Gun* was one of the leading money-makers last year in Italy. Woody Allen is a perennial critical success. And even a full-blown disaster like *Howard the Duck* finds fans and defenders here. But as a rule, all foreign films are dubbed.

Even for those Americans whose Italian is perfect this presents problems. No matter how much effort the dubbers take to synchronize the dialogue with the actor's or actress's lip movements, there is simply something ridiculous and disorienting about hearing Laurence Olivier speak with the pretentious upper-class accent known here as *erre moscia,* or flabby *r.* It strikes an American ear—and funny bone—as if Elmer Fudd were playing Hamlet.

Dialects that add flavor and variety to Italian dialogue often flatten out the freshness of American slang. Regardless of whether they hail from the East Coast, the West Coast, or the Sunbelt, all movie criminals are dubbed here to sound Sicilian. All blacks, whether street-smart, dirt-road dumb, or triumphantly middle-class, seem to be Calabrese. Successful businessmen, be they venture capitalists on Wall Street, hog belly future buyers in Kansas City, or real estate entrepreneurs in Arizona, are transformed into high-bourgeois Milanese.

But the difficulties don't end with how American movie stars sound when they metamorphose into Italian speakers. Just as often it is what they say that destroys the tenor of a scene, inducing hoots of laughter during moments of dramatic intensity. In the Italian version of Sam Shepherd's *Fool for Love,* where so much depends on the way the spare, gritty dialogue mirrors the austerity of the inner and outer landscape, one crusty cowpoke asks his girl if she would like a Continental breakfast of *cappuccino* and a *cornetto.*

In Lina Wertmuller's *A Complicated Intrigue of Women, Alleys and Corpses,* an international production shot in English then dubbed into Italian, Harvey Keitel plays a Neapolitan drug dealer desperately infatuated with a reformed prostitute who no longer loves him. When he asks what she ever saw in him, she says she fell for his body and the fact that he always smelled like the sea. In Italian, the former hooker tells him she used to love his pirate's chest and the fact that he always smelled like seafood.

For an American in Rome eager to catch a film in his native tongue, the choices are frustrating and few. Recently a number of video-rental outlets have opened, but their selection of English-language movies tends to be anywhere from two to twenty years behind the current releases. One can only watch *Annie Hall* or *Hair* so many times before one begins to suffer the same peculiar vertigo that comes with reading a six-month-old issue of *Time* or *Newsweek*. It's something you are willing to do to kill time at a dentist's or hairdresser's, but it's no way to spend a Saturday night.

The single theater in the city that shows a regular schedule of English-language films is the Pasquino, a shabby, threadbare place located in Trastevere between a lesbian bar and a deconsecrated church that has been turned into a restaurant. Frigid in winter, stifling in summer, ripe-smelling the year round, the Pasquino's daily program consists principally of movies that are years out of date. (*Tootsie*, *The Terminator*, and *A Midsummer Night's Sex Comedy* are playing this week.) But sometimes on the weekend it shows a feature that's a mere eight or nine months old, and this causes a traffic jam as lines form around the block, clogging alleys and doorways.

At such times, as one stands outside, assaulted by the elements, sideswiped by passing cars, and groped by importunate Gypsies, the tension of waiting to get in is heightened by the dread knowledge of what lies there. The seats are cracked and uncomfortable, the plumbing cloacal, the air fetid. The clientele usually includes a liberal sprinkling of winos nursing eighty-cent bottles of Frascati, or boisterous students and seminarians celebrating the end of the semester. The prints are often scratchy, the projectionist has been known to nod off and run the reels out of order, and the show occasionally ends prematurely due to circumstances which the management considers beyond its control. The electricity blacks out, the toilets overflow, or the ancient films disintegrate.

The Pasquino has a roof that rolls back in warm weather, and legend has it that a cat once fell through the opening during *The Way We Were*. Everybody who repeats this bit of apocrypha tries to authenticate it by mentioning the name of the movie that was supposedly playing. But one point is always disputed. Some people claim the cat was killed by the

187

fall. Others say it survived and attacked the screen, sinking its claws into Barbra Streisand's face.

While the Pasquino is the low road which the overwhelming majority of English speakers have no choice but to follow, there is for a fortunate few a yellow brick road, a veritable stairway to the stars. American Ambassador Maxwell Rabb and his wife Ruth regularly host buffet dinners in their official residence, Villa Taverna, a splendid sixteenth-century structure that used to be a seminary. Surrounded by seven acres of sumptuous gardens and marble statuary, the villa's driveway is lined by twelve pines representing the twelve Apostles, with Judas Iscariot at the end, slightly out of step.

When the dinner is over, Ambassador and Mrs. Rabb escort a hundred or so of their guests—usually a mixed group of Italian notables and statesmen, diplomats from other embassies, American celebrities, businessmen, journalists, and military officials—to a rustic building which has been refurbished as an elegant screening room, carpeted in deep pile and paneled with stained wood. The lights dim and —wonder of wonders!—a first-run American movie is shown in English.

Perhaps nowhere west of the Iron Curtain, nowhere else in the First World, would an invitation to a showing of *The Color of Money* be so sought after and constitute a status symbol of the same magnitude as a private papal audience or a lunch at the Circolo di Caccia. Similarly, nowhere else would inquiries about a film program prompt such stony silence. But the surest sign of the exclusivity of these evenings is that the Ambassador and the Motion Picture Export Association of America, which is instrumental in providing the movies, decline to comment.

When I called the American Embassy and asked when the screening room was renovated, what that building had been previously, how often films were shown, and who got invited, the Protocol Section responded with an across-the-board "No comment." Ambassador Rabb, I was told, did not think it was "an important thing to talk about the theater. This doesn't contribute to what the United States Embassy is trying to achieve in Italy." The guest list was "a sensitive subject," and so, while Ambassador Rabb was grateful for my interest, he refused to say anything whatsoever about the movies.

The Motion Picture Export Association of America was more tight-lipped than the Embassy. You would have thought I was digging for information about gun-running or state secrets. They would not deny that they provided films. But beyond that, they would rather be tortured with cattle prods or bamboo slivers than discuss what kinds of movies the Ambassador preferred to show his guests.

My contacts and friends at the Embassy, and a few journalists and industrialists who had been invited to movies by the Ambassador, agreed to talk . . . as long as we went off the record, on deep background, without attribution. I expected them to show up for interviews wearing E. Howard Hunt fright wigs and using voice distorters. I had to remind them that I myself had been to a movie at the Villa Taverna. So why this pointless secrecy? I knew the films existed. I just wanted a few details.

It was, they admitted, sheer self-protection. If the official Embassy policy was not to comment, they didn't care to violate it. What if, God forbid, the Ambassador got angry and dropped them from the guest list? Then they would be back in the line at the Pasquino waiting to see the sixth rerun of *Rocky II* or *Blazing Saddles.* They would rather lose their expense accounts or commissary privileges than find themselves shut out, scorned. It wasn't just the blow to their ego that they feared. They had wives and children to consider. Did I appreciate how tough it was for an entire family to go cold turkey? To go through life never hearing Tim Hutton or Molly Ringwald or Rob Lowe or Sean Penn speaking anything except Italian?

I did and I couldn't blame them.

They also urged me to show some sympathy for Ambassador Rabb. If word got around that he had access to English-language films . . . well, I could imagine the chaos it would create. Picture the fall of Phnom-Penh as portrayed in *The Killing Fields.* He would have thousands of American tourists, exchange students, military dependents, and expatriates clamoring at the gates to the Villa Taverna, all demanding to see the latest release. You just couldn't put a man, not even a diplomat, in that kind of a quandary. It was a simple question of triage. Those that were in were in. Those that were out . . . Sorry, but how did it hurt them if they didn't know any better?

Again, they urged me to think about the Ambassador and his wife. What if this caused an international incident? What if other ambassadors took umbrage at not being invited? What if, in the worst of all worst case scenarios, Rabb decided the easiest and most logical solution was to stop showing the films? You know whom it would hurt most? Max and Ruth Rabb!

A genial couple in their seventies, they were, in their way, every bit as full of fun and spunk as the President and the First Lady, and like the Reagans they were enthusiastic film buffs. True, they had never acted, but for decades they had had friends and business contacts in Hollywood, and they were fans of the first rank. No, they were more than fans. They were star-struck and enjoyed nothing more than watching a film in their private screening room with a few friends. Or, better yet, they liked meeting in the flesh those luminous creatures they had seen on the screen. They frequently held receptions for actors, actresses, and directors passing through Rome. Ambassador Rabb had once canceled his appearance at a celebration commemorating the fortieth anniversary of the liberation of Naples in order to attend a private dinner party for Joanne Woodward. That's the kind of starry-eyed, loyal fan he is.

No journalist likes to admit he would back away from a big story, especially one about the hottest ticket in town. But sometimes there are larger issues at stake—national security, America's image overseas, a man and his wife and their long love affair with the silver screen. Who am I to get in the way? I know I'd regret it. Maybe not today, maybe not tomorrow. But soon and forever.

Anyway, we'll always have the Pasquino. It's spring again and *Rambo: First Blood Part II* has returned. It's really not so bad—as long as you stay clear of the roll-away roof and keep an eye peeled for falling cats.

• • • • •

ROME, CLOSED CITY

Even for Rome, where theater of the absurd passes for social documentary, it was a strange scene that brought my daily stroll to an abrupt stop. A plump, middle-aged lady, dressed in a fur coat and high heels, was crawling across the rain-spattered roof of an Alfa Romeo. Her progress was impeded by a raffia shopping basket which she carried in the crook of her arm, and because of her stockings she couldn't get much traction on the slick metal. Her knees kept skidding so that she seemed in danger of slipping off the car, onto the wet cobblestones.

When she noticed me loitering nearby, watching with slack-jawed wonder, she shouted, "Is this your *macchina?*"

I told her it wasn't and went to offer a hand. But she wouldn't let me help her climb down until I reassured her that I wasn't the owner of the Alfa Romeo.

Finally standing on her dainty, stiletto-heeled feet, she straightened her stockings and smoothed her dress. With dignity restored, she explained her wacky behavior. "Some *cretino* parked right in front of my building, blocking the door. For hours I've been a prisoner in my own house. When the driver didn't return, I had no choice but to climb out and do my shopping before all the stores shut for the afternoon. Now I'll probably come home and have to climb back over the *macchina,* dragging my groceries. *Roma,"* she said, shaking her head in disgust, *"è una città chiusa."*

Rome, closed city. The phrase meshed with some inchoate notion I had long had in mind. No, it wasn't just a free association, reverse spin on the title of Roberto Rossellini's post-war film classic, *Open City.* I realized the lady was right, although perhaps not in the way she imagined. Despite its sun-flooded piazzas, outdoor cafés, and frenzied street drama, Rome is a closed city, and for all their superficial friendliness, Italians tend to keep their personal lives screened off, sealed in, secret. In town, their houses turn blank walls or barred windows to the street. In the suburbs, their villas are surrounded by high brick walls bristling with broken bottles or by fences of rusty iron spikes laced with thornbushes. They don't showcase their domestic affairs with picture windows or unprotected expanses of lawn.

As foreigners learn after repeated frustrations, Rome is often closed in other, more literal respects. Even natives have a hard time keeping track of the city's crazy-quilt schedule of business hours. While most shops shut down from 1 P.M. to 4 P.M.—the local equivalent of the Spanish siesta—government agencies, including post offices, stay open until 2 P.M., at which point they fold their operations for the day. Since commercial establishments reopen from 4 P.M. until 8 P.M., commuters must confront four rush hours —morning, midday, afternoon, and night. This effectively brings to a standstill those few streets that haven't already been officially closed off to traffic.

Over the weekend, one needs a Ouija board to work out the permutations. On Saturday, food stores are open, but hardwares, bookstores, travel agents, and airline offices are shut. If you want a ticket on a weekend flight, you have to take your chances, not to mention a long drive, and try to purchase it at the airport. If you blow a light bulb on Saturday night, you have to curse the darkness until Monday afternoon, when electrical-supply shops reopen.

On Sunday, flower vendors, bakeries, and newsstands do a brisk business until lunchtime. Then they call it a day and Rome plunges into a state of shuttered narcolepsy that Americans have difficulty fathoming. Forget about convenience stores or around-the-clock corner grocers. You can't buy food anywhere except in restaurants and bars—more than half of which remain shut on Sunday—and even prescription medicine and Band-Aids are in short supply, since only several widely scattered pharmacies stay open in the entire city.

On Monday morning, Rome reluctantly rouses itself from its coma. Groceries can be bought, but little else. Most stores don't go into action until the afternoon, and one never knows when a wildcat strike, a power shortage, a death or birth in the family, a bout of warm or cold weather, or some personal whim will unexpectedly shut down a business or the whole bureaucracy. I've seen bus drivers walk off, leaving their vehicles in the middle of bridges and intersections, and I've watched irate people bang on the doors of hotels and *pensiones* which, like prep schools or prison camps, locked up at 11 P.M. without warning guests.

As even the most desultory tourist soon discovers, what is true of Rome's businesses and public services also applies to those famous monuments and museums which are theoretically what attract millions of visitors here. As the *Galling Report,* a monthly English-language magazine about Italy, puckishly summarizes the situation, "Sometimes travelers get the feeling that Italian museums are some kind of secret society, a sort of collective Forbidden City. There are days when people feel that it's easier to marry a Cabot, or to break into Richmond, Virginia, society than to get into an Italian museum. Rome's museums are said to be the worst of the lot."

In the city's defense, it must be remarked that the problem is one of money as much as indolence or inefficiency. There simply aren't sufficient funds to restore and maintain all of Rome's archaeological sites, or to house its treasure-trove of art and antiquities. Furthermore, the municipal government has made considerable improvements in the months since the *Galling Report* noted that eleven out of twelve of the most important museums here aren't open in the afternoon and forty percent of the exhibition halls remain shut even when the museums are open. Still, whatever the explanation or the improvements, the schedule continues to be capricious. On Sundays and holidays, for example, precisely when most people have time to visit museums, they shut down half a day.

To add injury to insult, many of those parts of Rome which are not closed are enclosed. Walk anywhere and you will notice that celebrated ruins, triumphal arches, classical columns, Egyptian obelisks, and Baroque façades have been hidden behind chain-link fences, corrugated-metal walls, or elaborate weblike scaffolds that might have been woven by an immense spider. In some cases an entire building has been wrapped in orange canvas or green rubberized cloth to keep out the rain and sun and exhaust fumes while renovators do their work. The effect is to transform much of Rome into an invisible city as imagined by the late Italo Calvino or a vast shrouded artscape as created by Christo.

Eerie and uninhabitable as this may make the place sound, Italians are past masters at adapting to difficult conditions, and foreigners who wish to live here without suffering permanent culture shock or the emotional bends are advised to follow their example. Looked at a different way, the fact that the city is closed simply presents an amusing challenge, an opportunity to demonstrate style and imagination. For surely what is closed can be opened by someone with sufficient cunning and power.

Take the woman who was reduced to crawling across the roof of an Alfa Romeo. If she had had the right connections and ruthlessness, she could have summoned a towing service and had the miscreant's car hauled away and impounded. Then she, like so many of her fellow citizens, could have had an illegal steel barrier or a flower box as big as a bunker installed in front of her building so that no one could park anywhere near her door.

Confused by the shopping hours? Feeling abused by the bureaucracy? PO-ed at the post office? Fed up with finding your favorite restaurant closed? A wise Roman knows how to take direct action and triumph over these petty annoyances. He'll depend on family and friends, never faceless clerks or officials. Even if he doesn't enjoy diplomatic status himself, he'll arrange through personal contacts to have someone shop for him at duty-free stores, embassy commissaries, or American military bases. (An acquaintance of mine just ordered four thousand dollars' worth of stereo equipment through a member of the Foreign Service.) He'll entrust all his important mail to frequent fliers and corporate couriers. And whenever inconvenienced in the slightest, he'll call upon one of the dozens of food-catering firms, baggage handlers, delivery services, general expediters, and all-purpose factotums that form an infrastructure paralleling, and greatly improving upon, municipal facilities.

Even when it comes to culture—especially when it comes to culture!—there is what the Irangate renegades referred to in a radically different context as a "private channel." In part, it arranges the obvious: tickets to operas and plays that are sold out; invitations to art openings; introductions to famous painters, actors, and sopranos. But, more important, it provides a golden key to the most exclusive corridors of the closed city, and it has given rise to a phenomenon that can only be called Site Chic. Great prestige in this town can be attained by touring monuments, museums, and churches that are off limits to the lumpen proletariat. In conversation, one doesn't drop a name here. One drops a difficult-to-visit place.

In certain circles, for instance, the subject of the restoration of the Sistine Chapel ceiling will inevitably come up, and one will be asked whether he is for it or against it. Then he will be asked if he has seen it. Only a fool would say, "Yes. I stood there jostled by hordes of tourists and looked up until I got a crick in my neck and I can't understand what all the controversy's about." The proper, show-stopping response is, "Yes, I was up on the scaffold yesterday with a good friend of mine from the minister's office (unspecified). You can't truly appreciate the magnificence of Michelangelo's brushwork until you've seen it from six inches away."

Better yet, since so many people have been swinging like chimps from the Sistine Chapel scaffold, let it slip that you just got through climbing up the Arch of Septimius Severus. Or that you've had a guided tour of the dome of the Pantheon and you'll never forget the experience of gazing down through the circular hole at the top and marveling at the play of sunlight on the tessellated floor hundreds of feet below.

Best of all, somehow wangle your way into a site that has been closed to the general public for decades, a spot so restricted that only celebrities, visiting dignitaries, and famous scholars are allowed to enter with government-appointed docents. Silence silly persiflage for acres around yourself at a cocktail party by announcing that you have just returned from a tour of the Domus Aurea, Nero's fabled Golden House. Designed to please a sybaritic psychopath, it once had sea-water and sulphur-water baths, scented fountains, gilded vaults, gem-encrusted decorative devices, glittering mosaics, an octagonal hall with a revolving roof, and wall paintings by the aptly named Fabullus. Now it is dark and dank as a root cellar, and is deeply buried beneath centuries of rubble. One enters it as if on a spelunking expedition, wearing a hard hat and carrying a flashlight. But afterward one needn't mention these dreary details. Just rinse off the smell of mildew, search for a captive audience, and join the Site Chic competition.

Take care, however. The infighting can be ferocious, and there's always somebody in Rome who can one-up you or expose you as a fraud. Recently, I was—not lying really—

but dissembling, joking a bit and claiming I'd had an opportunity to visit a papal lavatory reputedly designed by Ra-
phael.

A young American snorted and said, "Impossible. At any
rate, the papal lavatory is nothing very special from an
artistic point of view. Read Anthony Blunt. He maintains
that the best Baroque bathroom is in the Palazzo Altieri."

"Have you ever seen it?" I demanded.

"No," the fellow admitted. "But I have an important
friend and he's working to get me a *permesso* from the
ministry."

• • • • •

MARRAKECH

Marrakech, Morocco—the mind reels; the imagination riots; the senses revel; the prose runs purple.

The city started a thousand years ago as a cluster of tents pitched by tribes from the Sahara who crossed the High Atlas range, then settled close to the mountains to escape the wind and to catch the water that trickled down from melting snow. Although it wasn't a natural oasis, palm trees eventually sprouted and formed a vast splurge of green on the arid plain.

By the Middle Ages, Marrakech was surrounded by walls. Built as if in imitation of the mountains, these ramparts still bristle with watchtowers and parapets, and picturesque as they appear, they served a practical purpose well into this century. The wealthy imperial town was often attacked and occupied by invading tribes and new dynastic rulers.

In 1912 the French imposed a protectorate upon Morocco, and colonial bureaucrats based in Marrakech tended to settle outside the walls in the Gueliz, or European quarter. The Gueliz is a replica of a provincial French city, with broad boulevards lined by cafés and shops, villas shaded by lush gardens, and courtyards cooled by fountains and scented with jasmine and orange blossoms. Foreigners lived well and cheaply here, and there was general tolerance for eccentric conduct and aberrant tastes. Gradually Marrakech became popular with artists with an eye for vivid colors, with writers excited by new experience, and actors who appreciated the dramatic landscape and equally dramatic local residents.

The life's blood of the town continued to pulse through the narrow, mazelike streets of the medina, and the city's heart remained Jemaa el Fna, a large, irregular-shaped piazza that quickens with activity late every afternoon. Even today, drummers pound out rhythms for dancers and tumblers; blind beggars chant verses from the Koran; snake charmers uncoil cobras from raffia baskets. Then in the evening as a breeze courses down from the snow-capped mountains and cools the sun-drugged city, lanterns are lit, and people crowd around braziers and caldrons that give off the smell of food spiced with cumin, saffron, and coriander.

To get an overview, I went to one of the rooftop cafés that surround Jemaa el Fna. The waiter who brought me mint tea was proud of his English and had a line of patter he might have picked up from a borscht belt comedian. "Berber whiskey," he wisecracked as he poured the tea.

I chuckled politely.

"Berbers are the Irish of Morocco," he said. "Always drinking their whiskey."

When I informed him that I am of Irish ancestry, he shot back, "Welcome anyway."

In loose translation Jemaa el Fna means "meeting-place of the dead," a most inapposite label for a spot so full of life. But in grisly days of yore, the severed heads of criminals and the pasha's enemies were displayed here.

These days a severed head is perhaps the only thing one is unlikely to see in the square. Everything else is available in abundance—beggars, cripples, con men, acrobats, Moslem preachers, palm readers, storytellers, and a benign-looking boxer who is willing to take on any challenger ready to pay the price. All around there rises the racket of voices and mufflerless motors, the beat of drums, the clinking of finger cymbals, and filigrees of flute music.

The buildings encircling Jemaa el Fna are a sundial of sorts: their color changes according to the hour, going from gold to ocher to rose-pink. As the crowd swarms in wide rings, wheeling from one performer or point of interest to the next, their shadows lengthen and interlace, forming patterns that cannot be rivaled by those found on Oriental carpets.

Coming down off the rooftop, swept along by the throng in the medina, I lost all sense of these patterns. The illumination was eerie, the distances distorted, every random glance into houses suggestive of some mystery only Max Ernst or Giorgio di Chirico could decipher. Bobbing along on a floodtide of Arabs and Berbers, I had a feeling that I was riding the crest of a wave, body-surfing past a profusion of merchandise, through distinct zones of color, sound, and smell. There were acres of fresh fruit and vegetables, hand-loomed rugs and painted leatherwork, brass trays and gaudy plastic souvenirs. In the meat market, cow and goat carcasses swung on chains like macabre mobiles. At some stalls, camel heads hung from hooks. Skinned down to meat and muscle, they still had their eyes and appeared perfectly content, as though unaware of what had happened to them.

Farther on, olives bobbed in buckets of brine; dates, nuts, and figs formed waist-high walls. In pastry shops, the soft candy and fruit tarts attracted bees which, drunk on sugar, eddied through the air like windblown yellow feathers. Lively barkers hawked false teeth, light bulbs, corroded batteries, expired license plates, and an astounding variety of amulets and good-luck charms—snake skins, flattened lizards, dead scorpions, rodent fangs, crab claws, and philters that could be fed to a lover to keep him faithful or to make him sorry if he wasn't.

◆ ◆ ◆ ◆ ◆

While it would be ludicrous to claim that Marrakech has not been changed by tourism, it remains very much a North African town. In an earlier era Berber tribes traveled in from the Sahara to sell gold, incense, ostrich feathers, and slaves. Now they are more likely to arrive by bus or motor scooter than by camel caravan, and they bring bags of charcoal, chunks of amethyst, and handicrafts, not the spoils of war. But the men still have daggers dangling from their waists, and they look regal in their turbans and djellabas.

The women are even more majestic. Tattooed with cryptic blue markings on their chins, foreheads, and cheeks, their eyes rimmed with kohl, they gaze out at the world with the cool imperturbability of icons in ancient Byzantine churches.

Berber clans are not the only ones who regularly return to Marrakech. No less nomadic, just as ornately made up, the international set migrates here every season, their numbers reaching a critical mass around Christmas and Easter. They travel by plane, often private jet, and arrive in their distinctive tribal regalia, the men and women both displaying designer labels—Cerrutti, Armani, Chanel, Kenzo, and Versace—as if they were catch phrases from the Koran.

While the indigenous tribes stay in caravanseries or camp in tents outside the city's walls, the international set settles in splendor at Hotel La Mamounia. Perhaps best known from Winston Churchill's paintings or from Alfred Hitchcock's movie *The Man Who Knew Too Much,* which was filmed there, La Mamounia is an oasis within an oasis, a walled enclave within the five-mile circumference of Marrakech's walls. Located amid thirty acres of gardens, it has served for more than half a century as an elegant watering hole for the rich. (During World War II, German and Italian POW's kept it in good repair until the carriage trade returned.) Its Moroccan motifs were always geared to Western tastes, and its heated swimming pool and pink façade were more reminiscent of Beverly Hills than the High Atlas. But for its clientele, La Mamounia represented what a hotel in Marrakech should look like.

In 1986, it underwent a complete renovation. Employees speak with pride and no little awe of what was accomplished. In less than six months, with nineteen hundred people working around the clock, all the rooms were stripped and redecorated under the direction of André Paccard. Like Egyptians recounting an ancient tale about the construction of the Pyramids, hotel officials rattle off statistics about man-hours, cubic feet of concrete, kilowatts of electricity, and the number of trucks, cranes, and artisans it took to reincarnate La Mamounia.

The result, to paraphrase Marx, demonstrates that a change in quantity is indeed a change in quality. But it would be difficult to say whether the new Mamounia is better than the old. It is simply different—bigger, brighter and less intimate. The original lobby with its beautiful beamed ceilings, hand-carved columns, and arabesque tilework has been turned into La Salle d'Honneur, where cocktail parties and receptions take place. The official entrance is an elaborate affair of fountains and pergolas and a broad driveway which resembles the showroom of a Mercedes-Benz dealer. Every model, from the 190 to the armor-plated stretch limo 600, seems to be on display.

La Mamounia now boasts a casino, a Regine's disco, six restaurants, six bars, a beauty center, a fitness center, a billiards room, a huge Jacuzzi, two squash courts, and two clay tennis courts. All 179 rooms and 50 suites have television sets which, via satellite, bring in programs from England, Italy, Germany, Holland, Switzerland, and Belgium. Video channels broadcast a daily schedule of movies in

Arabic, French, and English, and there is, depending on your point of view, something deliciously decadent or deliriously disorienting about watching an Eddie Murphy film while the muezzin calls the faithful to prayer.

The hotel is a full-service facility, and guests can—and do —check in for weeks and never leave the grounds. Many people freely admit that they come less for the marvels of Marrakech than for the sun.

In a sense, life at La Mamounia is reminiscent of a cruise on a luxury liner with an Art Deco decor. Faint strains of big-band music waft through the halls, and pictures of 1920s flappers and flivvers hang incongruously next to sepia photos of camel markets and Berber weddings. After breakfast, passengers—guests, that is—take brisk walks or swim laps in the pool to work up an appetite for lunch. Later they repair to the fitness center or squash court to get ready for cocktails. Then it's back to the room to dress for dinner. Friday night at the restaurant L'Impériale tuxedos and long gowns are de rigueur.

For those who do not care to sign on for an imaginary ocean voyage, other fantasies are available. The Winston Churchill Suite has the look of an English gentleman's library with wood paneling, leather upholstery, a statue of the great man, and a large ceramic bulldog that squats as if ready to sink a fang into any interloper's leg. Or there's the Avant Garde Suite, an extravaganza of glass, tubular chrome, extruded metal, and abstract art. Then there's the Baldaquin Suite, resplendent with a canopied bed that looks remarkably like the altar in St. Peter's.

For truly creative daydreamers, who reach Morocco only to realize that they would rather be riding the rails over the Simplon Pass, there's the Orient Express Suite, which is an uncanny imitation of a wagon-lit. It even has a spare bunk that folds out of the wall.

Of comparable opulence and considerably more logic are those suites with a Moroccan motif. The cordial lady who led me on a tour of these accommodations explained that American and European guests were more inclined to request Oriental rooms. Visitors from the Middle East and Africa generally prefer Western décor.

When I asked what sort of people stayed in suites, the lady responded with daunting candor, "People who have money."

"And power, I suppose?"

"No," she said. "If they have power, they stay in the villas."

She led me outside into the garden where three large bungalows stand behind high walls and thick foliage. Each has a patio, its own Jacuzzi, and separate wings for guests of countries where it is custom to keep a retinue of women apart from the men. Underground tunnels connect the villas with the hotel. "So that servants can bring meals from the dining room," the guide explained. She didn't need to add that these tunnels also provide security and serve as escape routes for the heads of state whom King Hassan routinely puts up at La Mamounia.

Last April, over the course of two weeks that coincided with the apex of the tourist season, Presidents Abdou Diouf of Senegal, Paul Biya of Cameroon, and François Mitterand of France moved into the villas with their advisers, wives, and bodyguards. This made for some extraordinary scenes of cultural dissonance around the swimming pool, where people from wildly dissimilar backgrounds gathered each day for a buffet lunch at Les Trois Palmiers. While the Europeans gloried in the sun and most of the white women wore bikinis or went topless, Moroccan security men with walkie-talkies prowled the area wearing starched shirts, dark suits and ties. Deep in the shade of umbrellas, the black women with the Senegalese and Cameroonian entourages sat swathed in yards of bright fabric shot through with gold thread.

The scene outside the hotel was equally jarring. Tens of thousands of Moroccans lined the streets clapping and ululating as they waited to welcome the foreign dignitaries.

Guests who had the misfortune to be away from La Mamounia at that time found themselves stranded for hours,
their return blocked not only by the crush of people but by
armed soldiers and policemen, who refused to let anybody
enter the gates to the hotel. When this unhappy fate befell
me four times in five days, I concluded that La Mamounia
must indeed be the most exclusive hotel in the world. Even
paying guests are not ensured of getting into their own
rooms.

◆ ◆ ◆ ◆ ◆

Villa Taylor is the most famous private residence in Marrakech, perhaps in all of Morocco. Built in 1928 and originally owned by a granddaughter of General Ulysses S.
Grant, it served as a U.S. Army headquarters during the
Second World War. In 1948, it was given to the Count and
Countess de Breteuil as a wedding gift, and with the death
of the Count and her son, the Countess lives on here
alone.

Surrounded by fourteen acres of gardens—"my jungle,"
the Countess calls them—Villa Taylor has, on the outside,
the clean lines and simple proportions of many another
Moroccan house. Inside there is a profusion of color and
decorative devices. The beamed ceilings are hand-painted,
the cornices carved into Arabic characters, the walls wain-
scoted with glazed tiles in some rooms and dark, varnished
wood in others. "Even to spend the money," says the Countess, "you can't do this kind of work anymore."

In the library, a red vest is draped over a chair, the phrase
"Capitalist Tool" embroidered on the back. The vest, the
Countess explains, is a gift from her friend Malcolm Forbes,
with whom she goes ballooning during the summer.

Although she is well over seventy and appears to be frail,
she is still a formidable lady. "To run a house here in
Marrakech," the Countess says, "you must be like this."
She makes a fist.

Just as she has the firmness and persistence to manage ten servants and deal with the often byzantine Moroccan bureaucracy, she also has the robust health to lead me up the tall tower that rises above her property. It offers a view of two courtyards, her garden, and the Atlas Mountains. It is the same view that Winston Churchill and Franklin Delano Roosevelt gazed out upon when they sat here chatting in January 1943, after the Casablanca Conference.

As we trudge down the stairs from the tower, I observe, "This is easier."

"Yes, as in life, it is always easier to descend than to rise," the Countess replies.

◆ ◆ ◆ ◆ ◆

Deep in the medina, Bert Flint lives on the far side of the city and at the opposite end of the social spectrum from Countess de Breteuil. A Dutch scholar and writer, he has been in Morocco for thirty years, studying the country's Andalucian heritage. His special interest is in rural art forms, and his goal is to "promote the creative continuity of Moroccan textiles. Tourism isn't all bad. It has given people work and allowed a lot of the crafts to survive. But it has also allowed the quality to decline. I want to encourage the purely creative side of the indigenous crafts."

He has collected samples of the best work from the past. (Pointing to his favorite Berber carpet, he remarks, "Aesthetically it is the equal of a Paul Klee painting.") And he has paid women in remote villages to produce weavings that express the full range of their talent, without regard for what will sell.

Bert Flint is also concerned about the preservation of the medina. Marrakech is experiencing a population shift away from the center, out toward the fringes of town, where the middle class is settling into new apartment houses and villas. Eventually the pendulum may swing back and people may want to return to the heart of the city. But Flint fears there will be nothing left. The houses here, constructed of hand-molded mud, deteriorate quickly unless they are periodically replastered and painted.

The notion is as intriguing as it is troubling—the idea that Marrakech is poised precariously between daydream and nightmare, that it might crumble like a sand castle and dissolve into the arid earth from which it was created, that for all its ferocious energy and fierce color it is as fragile as a desert flower.

• • • • •

REFLECTING ON HOME AND
THE ILLUSION OF PERPETUAL
SUMMER

"**C**ome back to Sorrento," the song says. But for years I didn't want to hear about it. I was more than willing to forget the entire Amalfi Coast. I had been there before, always with semi-disastrous results.

On my first trip, as an impecunious student, I traveled by bus from Salerno and crawled along the coast road clogged with summer tourists. Simultaneously transfixed by the beauty and terrified by the traffic, I couldn't decide where to look. On one side of the sinuous, narrow road, the land plunged toward the sea far below. On the other side, the Lattari Mountains rose in sheer cliffs to an elevation of over one thousand feet. Pastel houses clung to the cliffs like swallows' nests, and in every direction the perspective seemed wrong. Distances were alternately lengthened and foreshortened; the light kept changing; the colors appeared too intense, especially on the gleaming green- and yellow-tiled domes of the churches.

Yet it was impossible to relax and drink in the beauty on either side because of the horror that lay ahead. With horns blaring and tires squealing, cars and buses raced around hairpin turns. At times they shuddered to a halt, barely avoiding head-on collisions. At other times their fenders kissed as they passed, making a distinct metallic noise like that of a pebble dropped on a tin roof. There was no room to pull over and check the damage.

Opening a guidebook, I tried to concentrate on reading about Positano. The author claimed the village had been frequented by famous artists and writers. John Steinbeck was quoted as saying Positano "bites deep. It is a dream place that isn't quite real when you are there and"—precisely at that point I felt Positano's deep bite. As the bus careened around another curve, my suitcase fell off the overhead rack and fifty pounds of books, tennis rackets, and dirty laundry landed square on my skull, knocking me unconscious. I had to be carried off the bus like a load of lumber. When I revived, Positano seemed less the unreal dream place Steinbeck had promised than a nightmare that was all too real.

It took years for me to gather up the courage to come back. By then I was married and had two boys and had lived in Italy long enough to have developed a certain fatalism about the traffic. Starting with the assumption that it was best to drive defensively, I had learned that the best defense is a good offense. Keeping one foot on the accelerator, the other poised over the brake, one hand on the steering wheel and the other pressed hard at the horn, I tackled the tortuous corniche along the Amalfi Coast with the grim determination of a Formula-One driver.

It worked fine for me. I wasn't a bit afraid. But both my boys soon became carsick. The younger one vomited twice between Sorrento and Ravello, and we arrived just as dazed and bedraggled as I had on my first trip.

When I say I tried the Amalfi Coast again, I trust I won't sound like a masochist. Actually, it was with the intention of escaping pain that I drove south and discovered what I had done wrong in the past. The pain I was eager to escape was winter in Rome; the lesson I learned is that winter is exactly the time to visit la Costiera Amalfitana—when there's no traffic.

Before I expound on the second point, it is important to explain the first. Judging by the bland assurances of travel agents and guidebooks, winter scarcely exists in Rome. If mentioned at all, it is described as a few cool, bracing weeks between the glitter of Christmas and the bright glow of Easter. It sounds like little more than an excuse to drink an extra shot of gut-warming grappa or to buy that Missoni sweater you've always wanted.

But Rome has a winter that is nasty, brutish, and long. The last two years, there has been snow, including a blizzard (eleven inches) that paralyzed the city, transforming the Seven Hills into slalom courses and freezing the famous fountains. While, admittedly, that was uncommon, cold weather is no rarity here, and only the short memory of the local citizens keeps them from recalling this uncomfortable fact. To hear them talk, winter arrives each year as a surprise. Some people refuse to recognize it at all. They continue to sip cappuccino at outdoor cafés and eat lunch al fresco any day the sun shines—even if this means getting chilblains or watching miniature trumpets of frost form with every breath.

Perhaps they prefer to stay outside because their apartments are as icy as igloos. As I write this sentence, I am wearing a heavy sweater and a ski parka. No, I'm not on the windswept top deck of a transatlantic liner. I'm in my study. The air outside is a tolerable 56 degrees. The air inside is the same temperature, which is great if you're doing aerobics but excruciating if you're sitting still. There is a law here that central heating cannot be turned on for more than twelve hours a day. The other twelve, you pretend it isn't cold.

Or else you flee to the Amalfi Coast, which is what I do when I can't stand the damp, gray days that drag on in Rome until the end of March. This isn't to say Positano or Ravello enjoys a tropical climate. Only Danes or dimwits show up with swimsuits and expect to get a tan. But it is five or ten degrees warmer than in Rome, and the landscape lends an illusion of perpetual summer.

Nature has provided a sky of della Robbia blue, a sea that's a deeper shade of blue, and limestone cliffs that take on the burnished glow of the sun. Man has done the rest, terracing the mountainsides, planting them with palms and citrus groves and clumps of cypresses that flicker like dark candles against the lighter green of the other vegetation. Purple scrolls of bougainvillaea spill from balconies, and Virginia creeper vines turn fiery red as they die off during the winter in a conflagration of flame-shaped leaves. On even the dreariest day, the buildings radiate warmth and cheerfulness. Houses are painted in pastels or in earth tones that appear to have been fired in a furnace. Regardless of the actual air temperature, one is seduced into believing it is summer by streets that are walled with salmon pink, pumpkin orange, and Pompeian red.

But color alone doesn't account for the year-round feeling of cozy warmth. There's the beehive structure of the towns, which are all bunched in valleys or beside bays shielded from cold winds by the mountains. Once colonized by Saracens, the area still shows the influence of North Africa, and strolling through the labyrinth of streets—most of them blessedly inaccessible to automobiles—one has a sense of being inside an immense palazzo owned by a loud and lively family that has given you the run of the place. A piazza in Positano or Amalfi or in the vest-pocket villages of Vettica Maggiore and Praiano seems less like a public place than a private room where a party is in progress.

There is another reason why, in spite of my initial aversion, I now regularly return to the Amalfi Coast. It is a fine spot for a writer to spend time working, avoiding work, or preparing to work. Historically, it has also provided Americans with an excellent perspective from which to reflect on their homeland. For example, James Fenimore Cooper is said to have settled in Sorrento to finish *The Last of the Mohicans.* The local chamber of commerce has not made much of this fact. It prefers home-town boy Torquato Tasso, author of the sixteenth-century epic *Jerusalem Delivered.*

But I am fascinated by the idea of Cooper living in a villa overlooking the Bay of Naples. Poised between the Roman ruins at Pompeii and the Greek ruins at Paestum, he must have passed his days imagining the recent history of the United States, the country's brisk westward advance, and the forced march of his hero Natty Bumppo away from civilization, deeper into the wilderness. Then, after hours at his desk, he probably went out to a trattoria, ordered *spaghetti alle vongole,* and washed it down with Lacrima Christi, the wine pressed from grapes harvested from the slopes of Mount Vesuvius.

The thought of the laureate of the roughhewn American frontier living in splendor on the Amalfi Coast piques the imagination, but no more so than the notion that Gore Vidal has a villa in Ravello and spends almost half the year there writing about America. The grandson of Senator T. P. Gore of Oklahoma, Vidal has an abiding passion for politics that has more than matched his interest in literature. He has run for public office twice—for Congress in 1960 in upstate New York; and for the Senate in 1982 in California, where he came in second to Jerry Brown in the Democratic primary.

Though he now confines his campaigns to the written and spoken word, even on Italian subjects, he cannot keep from making allusions to his native land. In the two-hour TV special *Vidal in Venice,* he compared and contrasted the imperial Venetians to contemporary Americans. Interviewed about his work for Naples 99, a group organized to rescue the city that Italians have taken to calling the Calcutta of Europe, Vidal described himself as "a trombone" in an "orchestra of encouragement to raise money to restore Santa Chiara, et cetera. Actually, a bit of Santa Clara, California . . . Silicon Valley . . . would get the place going again."

Recently he worked on the script of *The Sicilian,* based

on the Mario Puzo novel, which Michael Cimino shot outside Palermo. The story is centered on the career of a real-life post–World War II bandit, Salvatore Giuliano, who was seen in some sectors of Sicily as a hero and who, among other goofy schemes, hoped his island would be annexed by the United States.

Vidal wryly observes that the hardest task any writer faces is "turning a hood into Robin Hood." But with *The Sicilian*, his job was made easier by experience. Three decades ago he wrote a play called *The Left Handed Gun*, which was made into a movie starring Paul Newman as Billy the Kid. Essentially, Vidal says, he rewrote that script, transforming the gunslinger into an Italian bandit.

With this, the cultural current appears to have come full circle. The American frontier that James Fenimore Cooper imagined during his days in Sorrento has returned to roost in Gore Vidal's villa in Ravello.

· · · · ·

FAR FROM CENTER COURT

Several years ago, while doing a book about professional tennis, I followed the men's circuit for six months. I set out with many misconceptions, none more ludicrous, I soon realized, than my assumption that since I was as passionately interested in travel as I was in tennis, the experience would prove to be doubly enjoyable. Although I knew I would spend much of each day watching matches and interviewing players, I imagined there would be ample opportunity for me—as well as for McEnroe, Connors, and Lendl —to visit famous museums and landmarks, lollygag in cafés, and sample the cuisine in celebrated restaurants. I was wrong on all counts.

True, I did a lot of traveling. That is, I took planes, trains, buses, and boats. But the journey didn't lead to a place. It led to a condition—a kind of claustrophobic fugue state, a fierce case of tunnel vision that leaves people on the tennis circuit with little time or inclination for cultural excursions. My life became a blur of interchangeable hotel rooms, sports arenas, and indigestible meals. Between matches, I imitated the players and spent hours staring into space, wondering where I was and why I was doing this to myself. Fatigue, boredom, homesickness, sophomoric humor, wild mood swings, a sense of living in a hermetically sealed capsule— these are the hallmarks of the international tour. If a camera is the symbol of the tourist, then a Walkman headset is the symbol of the circuit. Whereas travelers are eager to see and record what is around them, the typical tennis pro is obsessed with creating a placid inner environment where he can escape from all outside distractions.

I still like tennis and travel, and I continue to believe that they can be combined to produce a synergism of enjoyment. But I have learned that the tennis has to be of precisely the right quality—namely, the modest level of the game I play. Say what you will about the pleasures of being a spectator at center court, they cannot compare with those of being a participant in some out-of-the-way place, in some improbable match.

I am not singing the praises now of the thrill of victory or the tonic effects of competition and exercise. I mean that the mere process of arriving in a foreign city, finding a court —not always easy in countries where there are few public facilities—and locating a partner is itself an excellent and often amusing introduction to native customs and national character.

In France when one attempts to arrange a match, one is invariably asked, *"Comment êtes-vous classé?"* I am always tempted to answer, "I'm a middle-class American with certain upper-class pretensions and lower-class lapses." But such flippancy, I have come to learn, will not get me a laugh or a game. What the French want—nay, demand—to know is their opponent's ranking. In the land of reason and logic, every player from Yannick Noah to the lowliest hacker theoretically has a numerical rating. It is best for an American to claim he once held an assimilated ranking of *"troisième série"*—third series. This will convince mediocre players that they have a chance and good players that you will give them a decent game.

In England, where the best tennis is played at exclusive private clubs, outsiders are generally treated with withering disdain. It's not that one's athletic ability is in doubt. It's one's breeding. Unless you have a title or a hyphenated last name, the only way you will get on court is by exercising equal portions of imagination and daring.

Counseled and accompanied by an American friend who lives in London, I once bought a pair of baggy white cotton shorts and a shapeless white shirt, then took a taxi with my friend to the Hurlingham Club, where, needless to say, we were neither members nor guests. But we looked the part, and my friend faked the proper accent and line of patter. "Think we'll have time to knock up before it rains?" he asked the guard as we breezed through the gate and onto a grass court manicured like a putting green.

We played for two hours before it occurred to anybody that we didn't belong there. Confronted by an irate member, we admitted there must have been some mistake and fled.

In other countries, travelers eager to play tennis feel less like interlopers than adventurers or anthropologists or characters caught up in some farcical scene. Visiting Positano out of season, I once played on the tiny town's lone court, which is laid out on the roof of the municipal parking garage. My opponent was a plumber who doubled as a teaching pro. He arrived with his tool chest in one hand and a racket in the other. He beat me soundly in the first set and was sufficiently emboldened to make a bet that he could win the second set with a lug wrench. Sensing a hustle and imminent humiliation, I said that I would prefer that he give me a lesson—with a racket, not a wrench. He did what I asked, but acted grumpy and deeply disappointed, as if I had denied him a chance to display his full genius.

Isolated in a Spanish village, I tracked down the town's tennis aficionado, a bearded, soulful fellow with the azure eyes of a poet and the strapping build of a blacksmith. He played bare-chested, wearing espadrilles and a swimsuit the size of a slingshot. He was an expert in floral fragrances and had come to the area to encourage the natives to raise flowers that would render aromatic essences for soaps and perfumes. His art was unappreciated, however, and it hurt his tennis game. "The problem," he complained, "is that these people think of perfume only as something a woman puts on to attract men and keep away mosquitoes."

One summer in Egypt, I spent days looking for a place to play and finally found a court at a hotel which was supposed to be reserved for guests. But the pro agreed to give me a match during the dead hours of midafternoon when heat poured out of the sun like molten gold and baked the clay court to the consistency of talcum powder. Every footstep, every bounce of the ball set off an eruption of dust. Soon my eyes were watering, my nose was burning, and my skin was the color of braised beef.

As if the heat and dust hadn't been enough to unhinge me, there was a ball boy who had a disconcerting habit of darting onto the court and grabbing the ball while it was still in play. Barefoot, but dressed in the tatters of a tuxedo that was iridescent with age, he remained remarkably spry and kept himself cool by sticking slivers of ice into the wiry tufts of his hair. Although I lost the match, I felt I'd gained valuable experience. In the unlikely event I ever play tennis in the Nubian desert again, I have every intention of tucking ice cubes into the loose weave of my own hair.

In the even more unlikely event I have another chance to play against a princess, I hope I will have better sense and plead lame. Several years ago in London I was introduced to the late Shah of Iran's sister, Princess Fatima, who claimed she had read and liked *Short Circuit*, the book I wrote about the pro tour. Dazzled by her flattery and blinded by her diamonds, I listened as she went on to say that she was an avid player, and in the days before the Ayatollah Khomeini took over and declared tennis an insidious invention of the Great Satan, she had hit with Bjorn Borg, Ilie Nastase, and Guillermo Vilas.

In fact, she said, she had recently returned from Marbella, where she had been working out with Lew Hoad, a burly Australian who had won Wimbledon twice during the mid-fifties. The Princess explained she had been having trouble with her serve, but Hoad had solved the problem by teaching her to toss the ball higher. Now she was anxious to show me how much she had improved. Could we play tomorrow afternoon?

"Sure. Where?" I asked.

"Your club?" she said.

Fearing that my photograph might be plastered on a "Wanted" poster at the Hurlingham Club, I didn't suggest we put on baggy white warm-ups and take our chances there. But I knew somebody who had a key to Cadogan Gardens and I proposed using the asphalt court.

"A public court?" she sniffed.

"It's really very private. There's shrubbery all around it."

The Princess arrived in a chauffeur-driven limousine. She wore a fetching outfit by Valentino and carried a couple of rackets constructed of boron or titanium or some exotic alloy used to strengthen spaceships. But the surest sign that she fancied herself world class was that she had on a Walkman headset. Indeed, she left it on as she performed an elaborate series of stretching and isometric exercises. She kept it on even as we warmed up, hitting forehands and backhands. Screaming over the din of music drilling into her ears, she said she was ready. Only then did she remove the headset.

I went to the bench to towel off my sweating face and hands. A few Iranian emigrés had shown up to watch. One whispered to me through the chicken-wire fence, "The Princess has never lost. She will never lose."

I suspected I had been seriously overmatched and I marched out to receive serve hoping to keep the score close or at least to give Her Excellency some exercise.

As I crouched to receive, Princess Fatima tossed the ball high. Lew Hoad would have been proud of his pupil. She flung it a good twenty-five feet over her head. But then she let it drop below shoulder level before patty-caking it across the net.

It fell like dandelion fluff, and I had to lunge to get a racket on the ball. I could do no better than shovel it weakly to her backhand. But she didn't move, didn't even take a swing at the ball. Instead, she stood her ground and glared at me as if I had committed some slimy offense against good taste and fair play.

Princess Fatima performed the same pantomime of regal disgust whenever I hit a stroke wide or short or anywhere out of her immediate reach. She wasn't bad when the ball came straight to her, but she refused to move and she acted as if it were contemptuous of me to try to make her do more than stretch.

As we changed courts after I won the first game, the same voice whispered through the chicken wire, "The Princess has never lost." Minutes later, when we changed ends again, with the score 3–0 in my favor, the voice had become more vehement: "The Princess *must* never lose. She has suffered much sadness already and should never lose."

I knew what was expected of me and had no desire to cause an international incident. I was more than willing to lose, but Princess Fatima didn't make it easy. With her not deigning to budge more than a step in any direction, the pressure was on me to push the ball back to the precise spot whence she could wallop it for a winner. This entailed a great deal of running and retrieving, and just the right amount of pace on my shots.

An hour and a half later, I was exhausted, and as I congratulated the Princess for sweeping the set 6–3, I lied and said that I hoped we could play again.

Her nostrils flared imperiously. "Perhaps. But not until you've worked on your game. And not until you belong

to a club. This court is awful. The ball bounces everywhere."

With that she clamped on her headset and stalked to her
limo.

I was philosophical. It could have been worse. I could
have been beaten by a plumber playing with a lug wrench.

◆ ◆ ◆ ◆ ◆

A STRANGER'S HOUSE

I didn't set out to live long stretches of my life in the houses and apartments of strangers. In the beginning it was just a question of convenience and economy. But over the years my motive has evolved into a kind of compulsion in which professional literary curiosity and a peculiar species of voyeurism play reciprocal roles.

The syndrome started innocently enough in the late sixties when, shortly before a trip to Europe, I met a lean chic French lady at a cocktail party and mentioned that my wife and I would be spending the year in Paris. Moving by a slow and subtle indirection that seemed to mirror the sinuous way she walked, the woman revealed that she owned an apartment in the Latin Quarter which was almost always empty. "You're welcome to rent it. But it's only a pied-à-terre," she told me. "Not at all equal to your American standards." She made me sound like the sort of vulgarian who can't survive without color TV, wall-to-wall shag carpeting, and a Barca-Lounger.

To show her how wrong she was, I explained that I was

a graduate student in literature, on my way to Paris to finish a novel. I craved authentic French experience.

In that case, she said, her apartment would be perfect. Located near Place de la Contrescarpe, the address was drenched in literary significance; Hemingway had lived in the neighborhood. The cobblestone streets, the slate roofs, the open markets, the cheap wine and bread, the view of Notre Dame from her living room window—everything made it a setting conducive to creativity, she said, and she would derive deep satisfaction from the thought that, sitting at her desk, surrounded by her books and bibelots, I would produce a novel. Who knew? Perhaps one day a plaque with my name would grace the façade of the building.

We rented the place on the spot and agreed to move in at the end of the summer, after she had had a chance to prepare it for our arrival. Unfortunately she wouldn't be there to welcome us. She was off to the Far East. But she would leave a letter of instructions.

The letter proved to be a masterpiece of brevity. "Make yourself at home," it read.

But this was a tall order. The tiny place scarcely allowed room for us to turn around. Filled from tile floor to beamed ceiling with the lady's belongings, it bore less resemblance to an artist's studio than to a storage bin. The walls were lined with books, but they lay far out of reach, behind a midden heap of family relics, threadbare clothes, shoes run down at the heels, and cardboard boxes stuffed with receipts, recipes, and travel brochures. Open mail littered the desk-top, and next to the bed stood a mysterious machine which my wife believed was used to press ducks. I thought it resembled a medieval torture device.

It would be hard to say whether our anger exceeded our bewilderment. What had the apartment looked like before the owner tidied it up? What sort of landlady left her stockings soaking in the bidet? Considering the modest rent we paid her, why would she want interlopers trespassing on the most private preserves of her life?

Despite our bafflement and disappointment, we decided it would be more trouble to move than to make the place livable, and so we embarked on the task of sorting through the refuse of our landlady's past. But as we attempted to create some physical and emotional space for ourselves, the process turned out to be more complicated and involving than we had anticipated. In fact, we found ourselves swept along much the way one is by a fascinating narrative, and I ultimately concluded that it wasn't mere haste or sloppiness that had prompted the woman to leave her personal effects exposed. On some unconscious level she wanted us to know her.

Although I resisted reading the letters on the desk, I read the objects in the room. I drew inferences from her choice of books, magazines, and clothes. I speculated that she was vain about her hands and indifferent to her feet: she wore cheap shoes and expensive gloves. Judging by the kitchen's size and costly equipment, I guessed that she cared more about food than about sleep—if the spavin bed was an accurate index. I learned which scent she wore, which saint she prayed to—she used holy cards of Saint Catherine as bookmarkers even in editions of Genet's plays—and with whom she spent her vacation every August.

As I sifted the rubble like an archaeologist and came to a rough understanding of one French woman, I felt I was beginning to understand the French people. This was, I realized, the authentic experience I had said I craved, and it carried me deeper into the national character than I could ever hope to travel at that time with my shaky grasp of the language. This more than compensated for the shortcomings of the apartment and it prepared my wife and me for two decades of seasonal rentals, long sublets, sabbaticals, and vacation exchanges, almost all of which we took sight unseen.

Each place, even if stripped of everything save essentials, seemed to contain a personal message which with effort we could decipher. But in some cases, there was no deep mystery; everything was out front. The owner of an abysmal basement flat in London left a note explaining that she was an aspiring author and hoped I would read her pile of unpublished manuscripts. On a return trip to Paris, in an apartment rented through an agent, we were startled to find every flat surface, including large expanses of the floor, covered with negatives, contact sheets, and photographs. It turned out that our absentee landlord was the famous *Time-Life* photographer Ernst Haas, who had either departed in an ungodly hurry or, I prefer to think, decided to treat his tenants to a private exhibition of his work. Whatever his purpose, I spent two enjoyable months thumbing through thousands of his pictures.

The essence of other temporary homes and their owners was harder to fathom. One winter we settled in the south of France. By long-distance telephone, we had rented a recently built villa which was reputed to be an extraordinary example of something or other. The real estate agent had raced when he reached that part of his spiel. As I understood it, the architect was internationally renowned. Le Corbusier's name was invoked in a vague, breathless reference that reminded me of college roommates who tried to talk people into blind dates with girls about whom the best thing that could be said was that they made their own clothes. Only at the last moment did one comprehend that given the girl's size and shape, she *had* to make her own clothes.

Still, we paid four months' advance rent and put down a larcenous damage deposit, and arrived to discover to our considerable relief that the villa actually did bear many of Le Corbusier's hallmarks—wide windows, skylights, molded concrete walls, an enclosed courtyard, and an intricate arrangement of space into what architecture textbooks refer to as "a machine for living."

Unhappily, one basic amenity was missing: The villa lacked a heating system. By mid-November the "machine for living" had become as cold as a crypt, and in that jumble of concrete boxes we came close to dying of hypothermia amid the unavailing consolations of symmetry and clean lines. Hanging army blankets over the large windows, ruining our view of a landscape worthy of Cézanne, we shut off one refrigerator of a room after another and burrowed toward the center of the house in a vain search for warmth. But a cruel chill penetrated everywhere, and the tile floors felt like iced-over ponds. Finally, we had to install an oil-burning stove that smudged the whitewashed walls and fouled the air. We might as well have been living in a tenement in Gary, Indiana. As we transformed this marvelous example of modern architecture into a slum, I realized that whatever else you might say about a work of art, it was sometimes uncomfortable to live in one.

Since the villa's owner—who was also its designer and builder—had left behind no personal mementos that would offer insight into his character, I drew deductions about him based on the innovative shape of the house. I saw him as an aesthete, an ethereal type too absorbed by pure art to be concerned about practical exigencies such as heat. But when I met the man, he was less like the graceful outer shell of the building than like its inhospitable interior and I saw how wrong I had been to expect a pale retiring *artiste*. The man's creation was, like a lot of modern art, an aggressive statement, a challenge. He brusquely dismissed my comments about living in—and barely surviving—the house and demanded to know what I thought of its line and mass.

Naturally, after a few early mistakes, we cut down on needless trouble and developed world-class skills at coping with the unexpected. On several occasions we reached our temporary address and discovered that the owner had left behind more than a shimmering sense of his aura or tangible evidence of his occupancy. Indeed, he hadn't left at all. He wanted to stay on for days—weeks, in one case—and demonstrate the idiosyncrasies of the furnace or instruct us in

the care and handling of his begonias. Nothing, I feel confi-
dent, is more difficult than ordering a man out of his own
house, but we got quite good at it.

In self-protection, we also began to master the world's one
universal language, the Esperanto of real estate, and as part
of our vocabulary lesson, we learned that "architect-
designed" means "eccentric plumbing" and "unreliable
heat," "quaint" means "cramped," "quiet" means "accessi-
ble only by four-wheel-drive vehicle," and "folkloric"
means . . . actually, this definition requires some explaining.

I had always wanted to live in a perfect Alpine village. Not
for me the new European ski resorts with their tacky time-
share chalets and high-rise condos. A friend, an Italian
woman of Austrian ancestry, suggested I take my wife and
sons to Cortina d'Ampezzo. At one end of the social and
economic scale, she recommended the Hotel Cristallo, a
grand gingerbread palace with a panoramic view of the town
and the craggy, snow-capped Dolomites. Or, she said, if I
was interested in a truly folkloric experience, she knew just
the spot. She had often stayed there herself, as had a long
list of celebrities and Italian politicians, whom she named.
It was a five-hundred-year-old farmhouse run by an ageless
woman of great charm. The rooms were spacious and clean
and the ski lifts were within walking distance.

I called instantly and reserved an apartment for the
Christmas season, and when we arrived the farmhouse appeared to be everything our friend had described. She had,
however, omitted one salient fact. Tourists didn't have the
farm to themselves. They were far outnumbered by goats,
and these creatures spent the icy winter months indoors, in
a stable just beneath our apartment. Those familiar with the
smell of goats will not be surprised to hear that a noisome
odor had for centuries risen through the floorboards of our
rooms and insinuated itself into the warp and woof of every
sheet, cushion, pillow, duvet, and piece of furniture. Within
days our shoes and clothes reeked like *chèvre* cheese and we

227

began to receive reproachful glances whenever we entered a restaurant or an enclosed gondola.

After a week, we fled the redolent farmhouse. But brief as it had been, the visit to Cortina d'Ampezzo made an indelible impression on my boys. Now whenever we pass a manure pile or an open sewer, they breathe deep and sing out, "How folkloric!"

✦ ✦ ✦ ✦ ✦

EXPATRIATE

According to the dictionary, an expatriate is a person who has left his own country to reside in another. But this succinct definition doesn't acknowledge, much less explain, the dozens of disparaging connotations that have cropped up around the word. For centuries, especially in the United States, a faint whiff of suspicion, even scandal, has attached itself to people who prefer not to stay put in their homeland. Perhaps it is mostly a matter of pronunciation or misspelling —"expatriate" evolving into "ex-patriot"—which makes the word resonate like an accusation. Whatever the reason, generations of Americans have felt compelled to fight a rearguard action and try to convince their fellow citizens that they aren't disloyal or treasonous just because they have chosen to live abroad.

By now, the defenses have become as familiar and formulaic as the attacks, and the biographies of the famous, no less than the personal letters of the obscure, often echo with the same litany of justifications. Some expatriates say they remain in Europe because it has a more stimulating atmosphere or shows greater tolerance of offbeat behavior. Others take a practical approach. Artists and scholars, for example, explain that they must go where the light is good or where the lessons of the masters may be learned. More practical still are those who seek to persuade their commerce-minded countrymen that life abroad is essentially a smart business proposition. They have discovered paradise, they claim, at discount prices.

Cleverest by far are those who console the home folks with the excuse that they have stayed overseas only in the hope that this will help them arrive at a deeper understanding of the States. Performing an ornate ballet of paradoxes, they promise that the farther they travel, the closer they will feel to the family. The longer they are away, the more they appreciate their native land.

In spite of all the subtle skill and brute energy they marshal in their defense, there's little evidence that expatriates are viewed much differently today than they were in the 1920s, when Ernest Hemingway catalogued their crimes and misdemeanors in a stretch of satirical dialogue in *The Sun Also Rises.*

"You're an expatriate. You've lost touch with the soil. You get precious. Fake European standards have ruined you. You drink yourself to death. You become obsessed by sex. You spend all your time talking, not working. You are an expatriate, see? You hang around cafés."

"It sounds like a swell life," I said. "When do I work?"

"You don't work. One group claims women support you. Another group claims you're impotent."

It is little wonder that few people nowadays would choose to describe themselves as expatriates. Instead, living a life that dare not speak its name, they struggle to invent new labels free of past pejorative associations. They call themselves Trans-Continentals or Mid-Atlantic types or some other euphemism. Alastair Reid has spent more than half his life living in, and writing about, countries far from his native Scotland, yet he takes pains in his recent book *Whereabouts* to make it clear that he is not an expatriate; he is a "foreigner." As he describes the difference:

> The expatriate settles in a country for peripheral reasons; his involvement is with back home. The foreigner's involvement is with where he is. He has no other home.

An expatriate, Reid goes on,

> still retains, at the back of his mind, the awareness that he has a true country, more real to him that any other he happens to have selected. Thus, he is only at ease with other expatriates. They justify one another, as they wait about in the sun for the arrival of mail or money. Eventually, they are driven to talk of plumbing, the ultimate sign of the superiority of their own civilization.

I could argue with Reid and point out that Italy, my adopted country, often strikes its own citizens as more surrealistic than real, a kaleidoscope of random images rather than the sort of logical diorama one sees at American theme parks, which purport to teach the republic's history and heritage. I could object that although my Italian is seriously flawed, I find I have no more trouble following the discourse here than I do in the States when listening to politicians, computer programmers, or venture capitalists. As for waiting in the sun for money and mail, I would remind Reid that the European climate being what it is, one is far more apt to wait in the rain. But regardless of the climate, I know of few people anywhere in the world who fail to collect their letters or paychecks, and in my opinion, plumbing is a universal topic which serves less to assert the superiority of one's civilization than to dramatize the wonder and variety of human experience. As they express it in Texas, where I was an immigrant before moving to Rome, "Life is a funny old dog." I confess I continue to tell captive audiences at cocktail parties about the time I was in our bathtub and the water heater blew up and a fork of lightning-like electricity sizzled down the wall, then died just before it fried me. I do so not to denigrate plumbing *all'italiana*, but only to express euphoric relief that I survived.

Still, these are mere quibbles and I must finally admit that I am an expatriate. What's more, Reid is right; I do feel at ease with other expatriates, and my greatest involvement, personally and professionally, is with America, not Italy. While I settled here for peripheral reasons, I have remained for ones that are even more difficult to explain. There's no longer the excuse that Rome is cheap—according to the latest statistics it is more expensive than New York City— and after a decade I sometimes find myself less fascinated than infuriated by those idiosyncrasies that make the city unique. But I stay on and, ironically, part of my motive for doing so is the same one that constantly leads me to question whether I shouldn't go back to the States. I am referring now to my children. Half the time, I think I am doing them a disservice by raising them outside of their own culture. At other times, I'm convinced that I have provided them with opportunities of inestimable value. Still, since I've always intended to return, I wonder whether we shouldn't leave now before . . .

Before what? Before it's too late, comes the automatic and much too melodramatic response. And yet I cannot deny that I feel a sense of growing urgency. Perhaps what makes me most uneasy is a fear that Alastair Reid is right about another thing: There is something called a "foreigner," as distinct from an "expatriate," and while I'm certain I can reintegrate myself in American life, my sons might wind up as permanent inhabitants of a treacherous middle ground, trapped between Europe and the United States, not quite comfortable in either place, foreigners wherever they live. Worse yet, they might become foreigners to their mother and me, as well as to other people who are more firmly grounded in a single culture.

Meanwhile, as I grapple with these half-formed thoughts

and try to decide whether to leave and where to go, I keep a careful count of the advantages of living abroad. Both boys are bilingual and attend international schools whose student bodies appear to have been assembled in response to a Health, Education and Welfare directive. All races, creeds, and colors are represented: Christians, Jews, Moslems, Hindi, Buddhists, and animists mix on easy terms. In this context, foreign languages are concrete, living organisms, not just course requirements. Cultural differences are occasions for discussion, not discord. History is what surrounds them in the streets. Art is an integral aspect of their daily lives, and the new and exotic are what await them on frequent class field trips. Surely, I tell myself, this is a magnificent education, not to mention excellent preparation for life in a pluralistic society like America.

When I describe our lives to friends in the States, they say, "That sounds wonderful. Why would you consider leaving? Do you know what it's like to raise kids here?" Some go so far as to sigh and wish they could spend a few years in Europe. Yet I notice that even those not bound by jobs or circumstances seldom act on this impulse. Much as they might express interest in changing countries, learning new languages, or meeting different people, they stay put. Although they might occasionally criticize America or express general concern about crime, violence, and rampant materialism, they proceed on the assumption that home is still best.

On some deep atavistic level, I suppose I agree with them and I feel no small measure of guilt that my children aren't better acquainted with their country. I am especially distressed that they are ignorant of the myriad of tiny, yet crucial, details that comprise the mosaic of the nation's identity. My boys, for example, know nothing about baseball and football. When we move back, how will they communicate with other kids if they don't know the names of teams, the batting averages and vital statistics of star players, the records of champions? Later on, as men, what will they do during the World Series and on Super Sunday? And will

their neighbors and colleagues at work regard them with
stunned disbelief when they reveal their ignorance of other
assumptions, large and small, that Americans depend on in
the conduct of their affairs?

It nags at me that if we don't return soon, my sons won't
just feel like foreigners in the States. They'll seem as bum-
bling and befuddled as the tourists they have seen in Rome
—unable to operate a pay telephone, wary of cabs and
buses, perplexed by the currency, hesitant about using collo-
quial expressions for fear of coming out with some incred-
ible barbarity. In short, they're in danger of becoming the
kind of unintentionally comic character their own father
often is in Italy. They have had occasion to watch in acute
embarrassment as I believed I was asking a bank teller to
close my account when, in fact, I was inviting him to commit
an act of sexual deviancy.

They have also had certain slapstick experiences during
brief visits to the States, which suggest exactly how much
more basic information they need to assimilate. This past
summer, while at his grandparents' house, my younger son,
who is seven, pressed a button on the bathroom wall which
he thought would flush the toilet. That's how things work in
our Roman apartment. But he learned that buttons function
differently in Pittsburgh, Pennsylvania, and, in an incident
that dramatized for him rich new dimensions of the phrase
"culture shock," he discovered that he had set off an emergency alarm which automatically summoned a contingent of
local policemen. Much as my in-laws labored to explain the
mistake, the cops weren't satisfied until they had searched
the entire house.

In a way, that clamorous alarm has been reverberating in
my head ever since. It has crystallized the realization that
we must go back to the States. Otherwise my sons, having
mastered the quirky complexities of European plumbing—
pace Alastair Reid—might refuse to touch the American
variety. Yet the question remains, just as it does for every
expatriate: When to go and where?

Born in Washington, D.C., MICHAEL MEWSHAW graduated from the University of Maryland with a B.A. and earned a Ph.D. in literature from the University of Virginia. The author of seven critically acclaimed novels and three prize-winning books of investigative nonfiction, he has received a Fulbright Fellowship, a grant from the National Endowment for the Arts, and a Guggenheim Fellowship. Mewshaw has written for the *New York Times,* the *Washington Post, Playboy,* the *Nation,* the *New Statesman,* and other publications in the United States and Europe. A columnist for *European Travel and Life* magazine, he lives in Rome with his wife and two sons.